TABL_ _

Kill Devil Hills Library
East Albemarle Regional Library
Kill Devil Hills, NC 27948
252-441-4331

INTRODUCTION

Many individuals still observe cannabidiol as an intoxicant. In any case, that is a misguided judgment because paying little mind to the sum taken, it doesn't make high. However, what is cannabidiol and what precisely is CBD oil? How can it work, what is it utilized for and is it lawful by any means? The accompanying aide gives much data about cannabidiol and CBD oil.

The therapeutic utilization of the hemp plant was drilled 5000 years back. Meanwhile, 489 fundamental segments of the hemp plant could be resolved. Notwithstanding terpenes, flavonoids and other plant-based phytocannabinoids, appreciate a curiously high-financing cost.

Until this point in time, 70 phytocannabinoids have been distinguished in the hemp plant. The best known

Brad J. Simon

about these, the tetrahydrocannabinol (THC), is Cannabidiol (CBD), cannabinol (CBN) and Cannabigerol (CBGS). Psychoactive or inebriating part of cannabis is tetrahydrocannabinol, which ties to advancement action at the CB1 or CB2 receptor (endocannabinoid).

The non-psychoactive substance cannabidiol ties to various receptor frameworks. CBDDaher It is viewed as legitimate, well-endured, and particularly more secure, some portion of the hemp plant and is especially intriguing for self-medicine, for example, to smother mitigating, hostile to epileptic and against schizophrenic properties without creating symptoms. The utilization of cannabidiol appreciates expanding prevalence in a corresponding zone because of positive encounters reports.

CHAPTER:-1

WHAT IS CBD OIL HOW IT IS FUNCTIONING?

CBD OIL EXPLAINED

What exactly is cannabidiol?

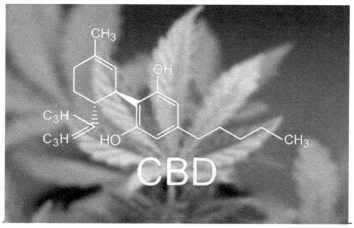

annabidiol is the oil of the female hemp plant. Since it doesn't contain the dynamic fixing THC or just in negligible sums, cannabidiol is likewise legitimately.

Cannabidiol is a scarcely psychoactive cannabinoid. In the hemp plant, it is available as the corrosive (CBD carboxylic corrosive). As it isn't liable to any lawful confinements, in contrast to THC, cannabidiol and a large number of its items containing the dynamic fixing are all the more ordinarily utilized by patients and pharmaceutical organizations.

Cannabidiol (CBD) is the second most significant fixing in cannabis Sativa (hemp) and diminishes extensive physical and mental pressure side effects in people and creatures (warm-blooded animals). CBD, not at all like cannabinoid tetrahydrocannabinol (THC), has no inebriating impact and overdosing with CBD is unimaginable. Indeed, even the WHO World Health Organization has said that it is protected to take CBD.

You won't get high on CBD because it doesn't contain any psychoactive mixes.

To give the cannabidiol its significant properties, mind-boggling expense and tedious systems are hung together for the creation. This serves, from one viewpoint, to meet the exacting administrative prerequisites in hemp handling under legitimate conditions and on the opposite side to serve the high and to be kept up quality gauges of the business and the client. Cannabidiol has increased monstrous notoriety and renown since getting to be mindful of its potential restorative employments.

Cannabidiol (CBD) is found predominantly in fiber hemp and by examination, found in THC (tetrahydrocannabinol) just in medication hemp assortments. While THC causes inebriation, CBD has no psychoactive impact.

CBD oil is a sort of cannabis oil that is for the most part cannabinoid CBD, and not at all like THC, it doesn't make it "high" or has a euphoric impact. The enthusiasm for CBD oil keeps on expanding, likewise in the media, as a result of its wellbeing advancing and calming impact.

HEMP OIL EXPLAINED

History and inception of the hemp plant

emp is exceedingly viewed as probably the most seasoned harvest on the planet.

Hemp has been developed for over 10,000 years and has been utilized in material creation worldwide for somewhere in the range of 3,000 years.

The hemp plant can be utilized from numerous points of view. 5,000 years back, China created materials and paper from around 2000 years prior. Numerous specialists effectively refreshing hemp paper, so Rembrandt recorded his first oil paint on hemp. Be that as it may, hemp has an alternate significance: Gutenberg realized it was an ideal solution for hypertension.

In the interim, hemp is viewed as a first-class item, for the most part, utilized for the generation of yarns, canvases, and pants. Pants are especially tear-safe because of hemp, yet additionally delicate and can be worn all-around easily.

Hemp has for quite some time been viewed as an extremely focused crude material. It was particularly important for the material and paper industry. The Krieg marine was additionally mindful of the estimation of hemp and utilized it for different purposes. The biggest maker of hemp at any point was

Russia, which secured around 80 percent of Western interest. Notwithstanding, with the mainland barricade started by Napoleon, England was never again ready to develop hemp. The choices were cotton and burlap.

Hemp is currently developed all over. The most significant developing territories are predominantly districts with a subtropical atmosphere. The hemp plant initially originated from Central Asia, where it was additionally significant sustenance around 10,000 years prior. The cannabis seeds were viewed as exceptionally nutritious and were likewise utilized in the restorative field for the treatment of illnesses, for example, ailment and jungle fever.

Around the twentieth century, hemp was progressively dislodged by manufactured strands however is currently on the ascent once more. The business utilizes it for nourishment, cleansers or paints. Hemp assumes a significant job in prescription, specifically, particularly CBD oil. It is utilized, for instance, in the treatment of sicknesses, for example, ADHD, wretchedness, Tourette and malignant growth.

Hemp oil is truly significant, sound and well-known vegetable oil. Cold-Pressed oil is flexible. Not the slightest bit is the oil gotten from cannabis Sativa, as dishonestly thought, inebriating. In any case, individuals feel significantly more agreeable after having some good times. Where hemp happens, since when it is utilized, how the oil is made and many intriguing actualities are gathered underneath.

The cannabis seed Cannabis sativa is the reason for the creation of hemp oil. As opposed to doubt, cannabis seeds scarcely contain the inebriating tetrahydrocannabinol (THC). This is in the pitch of the plant.

At the point when hemp items are made by refining the leaves and blooms of the plant, this is fundamental hemp oil. The THC substance is incredibly high in this methodology.

Advantages of CBD Oil

Advantages of CBD oil (cannabidiol) and why it isn't what you think

1. Alleviation of interminable agony

Brad J. Simon

The individuals who experience the ill effects of endless torment because of maladies, for example, fibromyalgia discover help with CBD. Taking CBD overt degeneration of the sensory system and can calm agony and even. It is endorsed in Canada for different sclerosis and malignant growth torment.

What is amazing is that CBD isn't a habit of resistance. That is the reason it's the correct decision for those attempting to avoid narcotics.

2. Alleviate youth epilepsy

CBD has against epileptic properties that have been appeared to treat medicate safe kids with the neurological issue, for example, epilepsy (no reactions!) Successfully.

Different approaches to consider: Childhood youth epilepsy is a genuine disease, and it is fundamental to work with a certified doctor who has practical experience here. Late research additionally demonstrates that a ketogenic diet can be helpful in medication safe epilepsy, for the most part in youngsters.

3. Decreases nervousness and wretchedness

As per the Association for Anxiety and Depression of America, 6% of the American populace is influenced by wretchedness and 18% of the American individuals from nervousness. Studies have sealed that CBD oil can support both.

CBD has been distinguished to lessen pressure and nervousness in individuals with conditions, for example, PTSD, social fear and OCD. CBD has even diminished the pressure and distress of general society.

Even though B12 inadequacy might be to be faulted, CBD has been appeared to bring down despondency by expanding cortical serotonergic and glutamate signals (both missing in patients with misery).

4. Battles the multi-safe microscopic organisms

The scientists found that cannabinoids (counting CBD) can pulverize microscopic organisms. An investigation directed in 2011 found that CBD can likewise slow the movement of TB in rodents. The scientists presumed that CBD would probably hinder cell expansion as opposed to antibacterial properties.

Notwithstanding the system for eliminating microscopic organisms, CBD has all the earmarks of being a viable weapon against anti-microbial safe 'superbugs', which are progressively turning into an issue nowadays.

5. Decreases irritation

Unending irritation is a noteworthy issue in our general public that adds to numerous no transferable infections, including coronary illness, malignant growth, Alzheimer's malady, immune system sicknesses, and the sky is the limit from there, as per the National Biotechnology Center.

Eating fewer carbs and way of life assume a significant job in incessant aggravation. Notwithstanding, if individuals are as of now eating well and nutritious nourishments and upgrading their way of life (for instance, resting and practicing accurately), the CBD can help. The examination additionally demonstrates that CBD oil can lessen the endless irritation that prompts the

6. Decrease oxidative pressure.

Oxidative pressure is in charge of numerous diseases these days. Oxidative pressure is the point at which the body has rich free radicals and can't kill them (with cell reinforcements). These days, it is a more concerning issue than previously, because our condition is significantly more poisonous than it used to be. An investigation directed in 2010 demonstrates that CBD oil goes about as a cell reinforcement, and another examination demonstrated that CBD has neuroprotective properties. In this manner, CBD can decrease neurological harm incited by free radicals.

7. Help with schizophrenia.

Schizophrenia is a convoluted and extreme condition that is normally treated with treatments and meds (which have genuine impacts). As it fills in as an account, numerous individuals have found that CBD oil has diminished mental trips. Likewise, the examination is making up for a lost time. A survey of the exploration accessible in March 2015 found that

CBD is a sheltered, compelling and well-endured treatment for psychosis. Notwithstanding, the presentation of CBD in clinical practice requires more research.

It ought to be noticed that THC, the psychoactive compound of cannabis, can build psychosis in hazard gatherings. Interestingly, CBD oil just lessens psychosis and can even battle weed incited psychosis.

8. Advance solid weight.

Cannabidiol can help keep up great glucose levels, reinforce qualities and proteins that help diminish fat and increment mitochondria that help consume calories.

The CBD additionally urges the body to change over white fats into dark-colored fats. White fat is the sort of fat we, for the most part, ponder muscle to fat ratio. Darker oil is a fat that is delivered in little stores and carries on uniquely in contrast to white fat. Dark-colored oil is said to improve wellbeing by improving the body's capacity to consume white fat, produce heat, and even control glucose.

9. Improves the soundness of the heart

Coronary illness is a developing issue today. It is one of the main source of death in the United States. Solid eating regimen and way of life are the principle needs for heart wellbeing, yet CBD oil can help. As indicated by the examination, cannabidiol lessens blood vessel impediment, stress-related cardiovascular responses, and may lower circulatory strain. It can likewise bring down cholesterol.

As of now referenced, CBD oil is reasonable for counteracting oxidative pressure and irritation. Both are the standard antecedents of coronary illness.

10. Improves the state of the skin

CBD oil can be utilized locally for the treatment of skin ailments. Studies have demonstrated that CBD oil has a high potential for treating skin illnesses, for example, dermatitis by advancing irregular cell passing. It can likewise help direct skin oil generation and decrease skin inflammation.

CBD additionally comprise of numerous supplements like nutrient E, which improves and ensure the skin.

Different Means to Keep in Mind: Diet is fundamental for sound skin. Numerous individuals find that evacuating nourishments, for example, sugar, dairy items or grains (if they are touchy) improves the skin. I likewise utilize a probiotic skin splash that has a major effect on my skin, powerless to skin inflammation.

11. Battling Cancer

The job of CBD oil in malignant growth treatment needs more research, yet the accessible looks encouraging. As per the investigation of the American Cancer Society, CBD oil may slow the development and spread of certain malignancies (in creatures). Since it checks oxidative pressure and aggravation (both related to malignant growth), it bodes well that CBD oil can help battle disease cells.

Hemp oil: solid angles

Numerous individuals wonder if hemp oil is solid and inebriating once devoured. In spite of the considerable number of biases against hemp or cannabis oil, it is one of the most beneficial sustenance oils ever. It gives the human body all the significant minerals, for example, calcium, magnesium, potassium, copper, and zinc.

It likewise contains nutrient E, nutrient B1, and nutrient B2, which are found in sustenances, for example, oats or oats and are basic for the body. It can likewise be exceedingly utilized as an enhancement dietary since hemp seeds contain the 8 amino acids fundamental for a generation. Hemp leaves have a comparable impact and can be utilized for a wide range of tea and without sugar drinks, for example, sound fixings.

The upside of hemp oil for angling

Today, every specialist is amped up for the wellbeing impacts of new ocean fish since it is wealthy in omega-3 unsaturated fats. Today, be that as it may, the fish is stacked with poisons and substantial metals because of sullying, with hemp oil giving a solid and earth agreeable option in contrast to omega-3 and omega-6 acids.

Great taste

Brad J. Simon

Notwithstanding the wellbeing impacts, hemp oil likewise has an impeccable taste, especially wonderful for biscuits and different baked goods. Can be utilized in the kitchen like any natively constructed margarine, yet on account of the flavor of nuts, it is perfect for virus dishes, for example, plates of mixed greens, cabbage or a wide range of sauces. Pre-cooked nourishments can be additionally purged by basically including them as a side dish in the wake of cooking.

Eat as opposed to smoking

You don't need to stress overeating or drinking cannabis oil because the body changes hemp, which is preferred taken by nourishment rather over hemp breathing in smoke from the joints. In any case, similarly as with all things, you should remember the advantages and disadvantages.

Therapeutic assistance

Indeed, even in drug, cannabis oil is incredible assistance supposing that it is adjusted, it lessens cholesterol, invigorates digestion, secures against joint inflammation and can help battle against Alzheimer's sickness and sadness. These entire unsaturated fats contained in hemp contribute not exclusively to a decent eating routine yet, besides, add to expanded cerebrum action, cell recovery and resistant framework movement just as hormonal creation. Numerous specialists concur that hemp oil is a sound and great dietary enhancement.

The substance creation and Biology of CBD: How it Works

CBD AND ITS MODE OF ACTION

Cannabidiol is one out of the100 known cannabinoids of the female cannabis plant Cannabis sativa L, which isn't inebriating. Because of its promising restorative applications, it is frequently used to alleviate indications or symptoms of more regrettable diseases. Additionally outstanding is its quieting, unwinding and pain-relieving impact.

Structure and differentiation of thc

The most outstanding cannabinoid is the THC (tetrahydrocannabinol), which is in charge of the inebriation of weed use. Like CBD, THC is additionally encouraging as far as its therapeutic application and far superior examined, however not relevant to a great many people given the inebriating impact. Since the two substances vary in their structure, they act in various courses in the body by interfacing with explicit receptors. OTC CBD items may not contain over 0.2% THC in Germany; so they are near without thc.

Brad J. Simon

Tetrahydrocannabinol (THC)   Cannabidiol (CBD)

THE ENDOCANNABINOID SYSTEM

Hemp research has prompted the revelation of a formerly obscure biochemical correspondence framework in the human body: the endocannabinoid framework. This framework, which has receptors all through the body, assumes a critical job in controlling our physiology and disposition. The real disclosure of receptors in the cerebrum that pharmacologically respond to cannabinoids and the distinguishing proof of endogenous cannabinoids that predicament to these receptors has essentially changed our comprehension of human science, wellbeing, and illness.

The truth of the matter is that cannabinoids and different elements of hemp can influence numerous physiological frameworks in the human cerebrum and body. Cannabinoids are substances that collaborate with the cannabinoid receptors in the body (CB1 and CB2). Among the best known and best-examined

21

cannabinoids from hemp are THC (primarily cooperation with CB1 receptors) and CBD (chiefly association with CB2 receptors). The realistic above demonstrates the circulation of cannabinoid receptors in the body. Notwithstanding the cannabinoids that are found in hemp, there are likewise (endogenous) cannabinoids such. Anandamide and 2AG, which happen in the cerebrum and the body all things considered and comparable impacts such. B.

IMPACT OF CBD ON SPECIFIC AILMENTS

Cannabidiol controls and balances the interpretation of more than 1100 qualities in our body that produce mitigating substances that normally restrain irritation in the focal sensory system and insusceptible framework. Since cannabinoid receptors are found in the body in immensely significant frameworks, they can push the body to self-direct and reestablish a condition of homeostasis. The scope of uses of CBD items is along these lines generally enormous.

Cannabidiol may likewise connect legitimately with the 5-HT1A serotonin receptor at higher portions, accordingly giving an anxiolytic impact. This G-protein receptor is engaged with a few neurological procedures such as — nervousness, dependence, hunger, rest, torment, sickness, and retching. The 5-HT receptors found in both the focal and fringe sensory systems trigger different intracellular falls of ambassadors that reason an excitatory or inhibitory reaction. CBD a (cannabidiol corrosive), the antecedent of cannabidiol present in the hemp plant (and in full-range cannabis items), likewise has a solid liking for the 5-HT1A receptor (much more so than cannabidiol).

ALZHEIMER

Neurodegenerative ailments, for example, Parkinson's sickness, numerous sclerosis and Alzheimer's frequently cause aggravation of the neural tissue. The utilization of CBD as a mitigating operator could help moderate the movement of this illness. The arrival of responsive oxygen is additionally run of the mill of Alzheimer's sickness, which is likewise connected with aggravation. At the point when aggravation happens, oxidative pressure happens. This decreases the cancer prevention agent limit of cells, causing the development of free radicals and the response with proteins and unsaturated fats in cell films. This prompts lost neurons and neurotransmitters in the cerebrum, which thus prompts memory misfortune and an assortment of other neurological indications. Since cannabidiol isn't just calming

ANXIETY

Aniety is promising to treat with a cannabinoid. In the mind, tension couriers are for the most part discharged by the amygdala. Cannabidiol associates with the GABA-A receptor in a way that builds the coupling fondness of the receptor for its endogenous agonist, gamma-aminobutyric corrosive (GABA), which is the major inhibitory synapse in the mammalian focal sensory system. The calming impact of Valium and different benzodiazepines (Benzos) is intervened by GABA receptor transmission. Cannabidiol lessens tension by changing the state of the GABA-A receptor to improve the normal quieting impact of GABA.

PAIN

Cannabidiol has neuroprotective impacts and furthermore demonstrates higher cancer prevention agent movement than nutrient C or nutrient E through connection with receptors in the cerebrum and safe framework. Receptors are minor proteins that predicament to cells and get a compound sign from different boosts and cells in the reaction support. This produces mitigating and pain-relieving impacts that help with agony treatment.

MIGRAINE

A conceivable reason for MIGRAINE could be an absence of specific substances in the endocannabinoid framework (ECS). Researchers have watched a few ECS instruments that could affect headache assaults. Anandamide is an exceptionally fundamental piece of endocannabinoids in the body, was observed to be altogether lower in the cerebrospinal liquid of patients with perpetual headache, recommending that this disability of the endocannabinoid framework in these patients may prompt an unending migraine. This lack could be cured by utilizing plant cannabinoids, for example, B. cannabidiol, which acts like the body's very own by invigorating the endocannabinoid receptors.

CANCER

Cannabidiol can even assistance with malignant growth by actuating PPARs (peroxisome proliferator-initiated receptors) situated on the outside of the core. The enactment of the PPAR-gamma receptor has an enemy of proliferative impact just as the capacity to trigger tumor relapse in human lung disease cells. Additionally, the cannabinoid alleviates the average side effects of malignant growth or the reactions of chemotherapy.

Principals Differences CBD Oil versus Hemp Oil

CBD OIL

The enthusiasm for the dynamic fixing cannabidiol and the restoratively valuable properties has developed amazingly of late. The cannabinoid is separated, and the oil is a famous dietary enhancement for expanding the prosperity and soothing numerous diseases. In creams or treatments, CBD has a wide scope of employment for skin disturbances and ailments, for example, psoriasis.

CBD is the second most common cannabinoid other than THC however has no psychoactive impact. It has been discovered that CBD can moderate the impacts of THC. For the generation of CBD oil, the cannabinoid is extricated from the blooms and leaves of confirmed hemp plants and blended with a transporter oil, for example, olive or hemp seed oil.

The THC substance of such oils is under 0.2%, so you don't need to stress over issues with the law. The extraction happens to utilize a supercritical CO_2 extraction. Under high weight, while the ideal cannabinoids are broken up by CO_2 from the plants. Throughout the procedure, the weight is brought down, and the CO_2 is the dynamic fixings once more. This jelly the common fixings. Presently, the won cannabinoids should at present be decarboxylase or actuated with the goal that they can create an impact in our body. They are warmed up to a temperature of around 135 ° C for a specific period.

In this progression, substances, for example, CBDa, which just happen in an acidic structure in the crude hemp plant, are changed over into dynamic CBD. The CBD oil likewise contains different substances, for example, terpenes and flavonoids, which give the oil its run of the mill smell and assume a significant job in the escort impact. On account of bearer oils, for example, coconut oil and other great oils, our body are likewise provided with profitable unsaturated fats simultaneously.

CBD has a different scope of employment and, when taken normally as a dietary enhancement, can have a different valuable impact on numerous infections and sicknesses. These incorporate various sclerosis, joint inflammation, provocative ailments, for example, joint pain, torment, queasiness, rest issue or psychological well-being issues, for example, tension, uncertainty, post-horrible pressure issue and some more.

CBD is one of the most encouraging cannabinoids, yet its multi-faceted impacts need further research.

Hemp or hemp seed oil

Hemp oil, significantly known as hemp seed oil, is gotten from the seeds of the hemp plant by virus squeezing. This kind of generation is most appropriate for this, as helpful hemp plants are fated for the creation of hemp oil because of the low THC content, the huge seed creation, and stable filaments.

The oil can have a green or earthy shading relying upon the preparing and has a severe, nutty taste. When handling unpeeled seeds, the chlorophyll gives the green shading, while stripped seeds are in charge of the dark-colored shading. Because of the high estimation of fundamental unsaturated fats, hempseed oil is viewed as an amazing top-notch palatable oil. Likewise, the fats arrive in an ideal proportion, with the goal that they can ideally process our body.

Since our bodies can't deliver them ourselves, polyunsaturated unsaturated fats must be retained through the eating routine. This makes hemp oil an amazing homegrown choice to fish oil. Nonetheless, hempseed oil isn't reasonable for searing or profound broiling because the unsaturated fats decay at a temperature of more than 165 ° C. Hemp oil is likewise

Brad J. Simon

as of now the most mainstream bearer for CBD - from which then the CBD oil is created.

Conclusion

While CBD oil is utilized as a dietary enhancement fundamentally for its therapeutic potential, hemp oil is a mainstream and astounding palatable oil, which assumes a significant job in a sound and cognizant eating regimen. Another distinction is the assembling procedure.

USE OF HEMP OIL

100 g hemp oil contains on average:	
nutrient	amount
calories	879 kcal (3,680 kJ)
fat content	100 g
Saturated fatty acids	11 g
Unsaturated fatty acids	89 g
Monounsaturated fatty acids	14 g
Polyunsaturated fatty acids	75 g
cholesterol	0 mg
sodium	0 mg
carbohydrates	0 g
dietary fiber	0 g
sugar	0 g
protein	0 g
smoke point	from 120 ° C

Ignoring the restorative segment of the hemp plant and its viability in the treatment of different determinations, for example, various sclerosis, paraplegia, torment, loss of craving, AIDS and malignancy, reactions of chemotherapy, coronary illness, queasiness, regurgitating, waterfalls, epilepsy, asthma, Movement issue, withdrawal manifestations, despondency and various ailments not treated in detail, so still stay in hemp oil innumerable different applications with healthy impact.

Fields of the utilization of hemp oil

The hemp plant has been holy to mankind for a long time. Their adaptable use, regardless of whether as rope, sack or garments, as nourishment and medication for people and creatures, or as an intoxicant for profound customs and celebrations made the hemp a fixed piece of our predecessors ' lives, and the well known Indians' tranquility pipe contained among others mind-extending substances additionally hemp.

Until the mid-twentieth-century hemp development was advanced around the world, in Austria, for instance, the government provided a guideline on the base grounds of hemp. Cigarettes with a dumbfounding completion were promoted straightforwardly and notwithstanding for the whistle-smoking granddad, the hemp was still a piece of regular day to day existence, which was given no unique thought, hemp use was typical. The rise of the plastics business prompted dishonest criminalization crusades by the halls behind them, which progressively and effectively dislodged the common item hemp from the market. The dread of the precluded medication and its fiendish impacts is regularly still somewhere down in the brains of numerous individuals today.

Hemp oil for the skin

Unsaturated fats proportion in fundamental hemp oil (3: 1) is nearly equivalent to the unsaturated fat example of human skin (4: 1), a biochemical condition that no other realized oil has. Quickly mix the property into the pores and in this way purge, detoxify and balance the skin tone. Since the oil of cannabis seeds, which are gotten from cannabis Sativa, the sans THC hemp, is practically indistinguishable from human lipids, it likewise keeps further skin layers supple. For every one of these reasons, it is especially powerful against lack of hydration and skin popping and reestablishes skin lipids. The gamma-linolenic corrosive (GLA) is utilized principally in the treatment of skin infections, for example, atopic dermatitis or psoriasis, additionally bolsters hemp oil scar recuperating.

The skin can be influenced by numerous variables in day by day life: dry warming air, unreasonable utilization of exceedingly degreasing cleansers, shower gels or shower items, yet also stress and the regular utilization of make-up and other concoction beauty care products adversely influence the skin. An age-related lull of cell digestion or diabetes builds the defatting and water loss of the skin. Here hemp oil can be utilized inside and remotely and along these lines gives a twice as helpful impact. This reality has been known to mankind for centuries, the delightful Cleopatra is presumably the most acclaimed, however in no way, shape or forms the main client in mankind's history.

Hemp oil in atopic dermatitis

Atopic dermatitis is related with a pestering tingling, which can be unsavory, particularly around evening time. Particularly babies and little children frequently experience the ill effects of the spurts of this atopic dermatitis, the primary manifestations of which are as flaky, once in a while sobbing, red changes of the skin and joined by solid tingling. Restless evenings regularly influence kids and guardians. Atopic dermatitis is viewed as uncorrectable in traditional prescription yet is dealt with. A broadly utilized technique for treatment is mostly restricted to the control of the trademark skin dryness by the outer utilization of mitigating operators, for example, cortisone, however, this can get significant dangers the long haul use. The explanation behind atopic dermatitis is an absence of polyunsaturated unsaturated fats, which by and large control water misfortune through the skin. The researchers found that oral organization of gamma-linolenic corrosive is effective in atopic dermatitis. Patients who ingested hemp oil through nourishment, connected it to the influenced regions of the skin and furthermore utilized it as a cleanser and shower added substance, accomplished shockingly positive outcomes and were eager.

Hemp oil for the hair

Hemp oil is perfect for improving the substance of the scalp and hair. It additionally ensures against negative natural impacts and has substantiated itself, particularly in dandruff and dry scalp, which can likewise happen because of stress, hemp oil has demonstrated phenomenal. For use as a cleanser, you can essentially blend it with (hemp) cleanser and water, as a conditioner, a tablespoon of hemp oil is rubbed into the scalp and the rest of the oil with a brush to the tips dispersed. After around 20 minutes of presentation, it will wash out once more, ideally with custom made hemp oil cleanser. On the off chance that you don't have room schedule-wise and relaxation to make your hemp cleanser or hemp cleanser yourself, there are brilliant items to purchase in the market, some of which additionally scented with alluring aromas.

Hemp oil for the dog

An infusion of hemp oil encourages the pooch to solid skin and glossy coat. Veterinary field reports have demonstrated that the utilization of hemp oil stimulatingly affects more seasoned mutts and shows extraordinary outcomes even on account of weakening and shortcoming. Indeed, even steady acid reflux could be overseen by directing hemp oil, controlling patient peristalsis and normalizing. Beneficial outcomes could likewise be accomplished in Arthritis and joint issues and even degenerative hip dysplasia.

Hemp oil for the pony

Particularly old, skinny and substantial ponies profit by the expansion of hemp oil in the feed. From one perspective, the nutty taste of hemp oil appears to taste ponies great; then again, it has a tantalizing and adjusting impact. Especially the difference in coat regularly causes issues for more seasoned ponies, with hemp oil an improvement of the general condition and a recovering of the coat sparkle could be enlisted a little while later. Hemp oil additionally positively affects foot development and horn arrangement.

Besides, constructive outcomes on the equine metabolic disorder (Cushing) have been accounted for. On the off chance that you need to complete some help for your steed, you can set up a "serving of mixed greens" of carrots, apple juice vinegar, and hemp oil. Not traditionally delivered, common apple juice vinegar has a reviving impact,

Hemp oil for hormonal issue and

Brad J. Simon
hypertension

The gamma-linoleic corrosive contained in hemp oil additionally helps on account of the hormonal issue, for example, those that happen in menopausal ladies or when there are standard grumblings. Indeed, even with hypertension, the admission of hemp oil has been demonstrated. Individuals living with hypertension are additionally at an expanded danger of stroke or arteriosclerosis. The negative, high-fat eating regimen of our scopes moreover supports the unsafe impacts. Ordinary utilization of hemp oil and a broad renunciation of creature fats can do some amazing things here. Likewise, the crabbiness related with hypertension can be settled by the quieting impact of hemp in joy.

Hemp oil for interminable irritation

Specialists at the ETH Zurich and the University of Bonn have demonstrated that hemp oil represses aggravation by inspecting an up to this point disregarded part in the fundamental oil of the cannabis plant and in doing as such finding wonderful pharmacological angles. The renowned logical diary PNAS as of late distributed new viewpoints for the anticipation and treatment of aggravation by managing hemp oil, which focuses on the tissue CB2 receptor and the related endocannabinoid framework, which have a significant job in the concealment of irritation.

Hemp oil for disease

Especially amazing, despite the fact that not yet completely examined, are the outcomes that could be accomplished in different malignancies. Here, elective treatment strategies and the necessities of traditional medication frequently impact. Self-investigations of urgent in light of the fact that effectively blessed to the demise of such positive outcomes, that the science wound up mindful. Various investigations have demonstrated that THC, the psychoactive element of the hemp plant, can hinder tumors development. The Rostock pharmacologist Burkhard Hinz burst tumors cells with a cannabis particle in the research center test.

Brad J. Simon

In Israel, the impact of various cannabis strains on tumors cells is as of now being researched. Instances of skin malignancy, bosom disease, and lung disease have additionally been accounted for to have been restored through remedial help with cannabis oil. Here, the pharmaceutical business additionally is by all accounts kicking off something new. Late licenses, which ought to be connected for certain hemp assortments, are the best evidence of this.

Hemp oil for premenstrual disorder (PMS)

Premenstrual disorder (PMS) happens in numerous ladies before the beginning of menstrual draining and is described by emotional episodes, melancholy, and crabbiness, a delicacy in the chest and guts, and general muscle pressure. As per contemplates, ladies with PMS have a lipid digestion issue that hinders the change of linoleic corrosive into gamma-linolenic corrosive. Here, a day by day admission of around five milliliters of hemp oil could essentially improve the indications. Additionally, the state of mind upgrading impact could be demonstrated. It has been uncovered to men that hemp protein is additionally connected with intensity improving impacts because of its especially high estimation of the amino corrosive L-arginine.

Can CBD help you q uit smoking?

As indicated by another WHO study, tobacco is as yet the major preventable reason for death on the planet, executing somewhere in the range of 6 million individuals every year and causing financial misfortunes evaluated at over a large portion of a trillion dollars. Numerous investigations distributed in biomedical diaries demonstrate that CBD can treat fixation. Specifically, two examinations in the UK demonstrate that CBD can help individuals stop cigarettes smoking.

With the expanding ubiquity of CBD to treat enslavement, individuals have discovered that it can likewise be an incredible option in contrast to smoking.

How can it work?

The truth of the matter is that smoking end is more than defeating physical reliance; it is additionally the procedure of propensity breaking, which is troublesome and can cause much worry for the needy smoker. Smoking CBD-rich blooms or vaping a CBD-

E liquid could lessen both pressure and tension and the propensity for smoking. The way that CBD can likewise normally lessen fears and add to unwinding is an additional advantage to helping individuals beat this propensity.

How to Use CBD to Stop Smoking?

Utilizing cannabis to quit smoking cigarettes is the same old thing. For a considerable length of time, numerous individuals have been effectively utilizing cannabis as an option in contrast to cigarette smoking. Both THC and CBD have a loosening up impact. In any case, everyday smoking of THC isn't reasonable for some individuals. It is imperative to realize that CBD is certainly not a psychoactive compound from the cannabis plant. Since you can't get high on it, it's an extraordinary option in contrast to utilizing high THC cannabis. It is reasonable for regular use and notwithstanding for work.

CBD oil is gotten from hemp at 0.3 percent THC or less and is accessible in many nations around the globe. There are numerous approaches to purchase CBD items to stop smoking; all of CBD oils, glues or e-fluids that you can vaporize.

A large number of the best smoking discontinuance methods incorporate supplanting your smoking propensities with new, more advantageous propensities, for example, a stroll after supper or some tea when you, as a rule, have a cigarette. Supplanting cigarettes with CBD is definitely not a long haul arrangement, however, it can encourage the change.

Studies have additionally demonstrated that taking CBD can help addicts who are likewise taking different substances, for example, narcotics and cocaine.

Can CBD help with diabetes?

The clinical picture of diabetes

The reason for diabetes is distinguished in the pancreas. There is the body's substance insulin (polypeptide hormone). Insulin is in charge of taking glucose (sugar) into our body. In the event that insulin discharge is impeded or seriously weakened, it is called diabetes of the glucose. Patients ought to intermittently check their glucose levels by utilizing blood tests taken to avoid the beginning of this illness. Uncertain, these assaults generally lead to finish loss of cognizance, including total organ disappointment.

Diabetes can be ordered into two classifications. Once in Type1 and Type2. Here is a qualification between the causes and the reason for the illness. Frequently an eating regimen high in fat and liquor abuse are in charge of the sickness. In any case, even the immune system capacity can prompt this diabetes. Analyzed diabetes of whatever sort, might be dealt with and blocked well by insulin infusion. Be that as it may, the patient must leave with specific impediments.

In sort 1 diabetes, the pancreas is excited, which emphatically influences the creation of insulin. Since CBD has a mitigating property, the medication can locate its mending application practically directly here. On the off chance that the irritation is back, the pancreas can likewise continue insulin creation. So researchers have presumed that CBD can even completely fix type 1 diabetes totally.

It has additionally been built up that CBD may likewise healingly affect type 2 diabetes. This kind of diabetes is generally connected with circulatory issue and fiery episodes in the venous arrangement of our body. This, thus, happens in agonizing just as noticeably appalling zones of the skin. The legs and lower legs are generally influenced. Once more, the CBD may fundamentally have a recuperating impact. Particularly aggravation and circulatory issue fall under the expansive range of activity of cannabidiol.

Likewise, CBD may likewise focus on the reasons for stoutness. Hence, CBD not just positively affects the whole stomach related framework yet can likewise decidedly influence digestion. This is identified with the way that CBD can go about as a hunger suppressant if there should be an occurrence of overweight.

Other than the positive and autonomous reports for patients found on the Internet, there is another fascinating investigation. It was completed by the National Institutes of Health of the United States (Bethesda). It was discovered that CBD likewise decreased cell demise. This passing is the reason for irritation, which can just create through diabetes.

Brad J. Simon
Significant for the impact of CBD oil in diabetics

The fundamental issue of each diabetic is that the pancreas does not create enough insulin. Thusly, the body can't ship the sugar from the blood into the body tissue. The acclaimed analyst, Dr. Raphael Mechoulam and pioneer of the CBD, found that CBD can likewise influence the pancreas and its insulin creation.

Enlivened by him, the examination proceeded at Hadassah Hebrew University in Jerusalem, where it understood that CBD oil could avoid the improvement of sort 1 diabetes. Additionally, the capacity of the veins in sort 2 diabetes can be improved by CBD oil. These are the outstanding advantages of CBD oil, who realizes what the specialists still discover benefits.

Worth thinking about CBD oil and diabetes

There is no such imaginative, and expansive based arrangement that positively affects such a large number of maladies, as CBD is all around consumed by our ECS framework and the dynamic fixing can be moved to the required area in the body.

Likewise, cannabis has a metabolic impact, which enables our body to process calories quicker and all the more proficiently.

Add to that the mitigating and pain-relieving properties, CBD oil is uncommon, as it can have such a large number of constructive outcomes simultaneously.

Likewise, they ought to consistently focus on quality when purchasing, which is normally connected with a more expensive rate.

Heart issues

The heart is the life-supporting engine for practically all living creatures. On the off chance that the heart is sick, this leads untreated to the constrained personal satisfaction or even passing. Obvious heart issues, in spite of the fact that the term sounds innocuous, ought to in this manner consistently and promptly be analyzed by a master. Today we are committed to the point: Can CBD help with heart issues?

Heart issues - the clinical picture

A dreary sting in the chest or a continually fluctuating course just as the unexpected pulling in the left upper arm - these can be the primary indications of coronary illness. However, heart issues can likewise go unnoticed or happen. So we regularly don't see that our heart likes to overlook the cadence or here and there beat it flimsier or more grounded. It ought to be referenced that (hypertension) has literally nothing to do with the heart.

One of the most notable heart issues, for instance, is the atrial fibrillation. Our heart works superbly; it's a vigorous motor. In any case, it is similarly as helpless or touchy. Heart issues can create over the span of life, or they are intrinsic. Heart issues can have numerous causes: beginning with an unfortunate way of life, enduring worry, to incendiary illnesses, for example, a non-relieved virus.

Will CBD help with heart issues?

In spite of the fact that it is critical to explain the idea of heart issues ahead of time, CBD might be a potential method for lightening the manifestations of minor coronary illness. CBD can have an exceptionally beneficial outcome on heart issues from numerous points of view. Similarly as unpredictable as our heart and circulatory framework seems to be, so too is the wide range of CBD.

Coronary illness can have innumerable causes. Aside from inborn coronary illness, the reasons for heart issues can be a basic cold, stoutness, or mental pressure. On the off chance that an irritation loads the heart muscle, cannabidiol can have a mitigating impact. In the event that the reason is heftiness, CBD may get thinner. In the event that the reason for heart issues is because of a circulatory issue, CBD may extend the supply routes.

In any case, if the reason is brought about by psychological sickness, for example, steady pressure or melancholy, cannabidiol demonstrates to be a promising cure here also. Besides, CBD can likewise act prophylactically. This is implied that numerous heart issues can regularly be the aftereffect of different anomalies in our body and way of life. These incorporate smoking, awful nourishment, or liquor. Customary utilization of cannabidiol can avert aggravation and mental pressure, or smother it in the bud.

When all is said in done, CBD beneficially affects the body and psyche. It is essential to make reference to that CBD is simply plant-based and does not cause inebriation. Numerous heart patients have detailed that CBD is incredibly strong of recuperation as an associative prescription. Up until now, CBD has not known some other symptoms or reactions.

Obviously, heart issues can likewise be brought about by huge medication misuse. Once more, CBD is by all accounts a potential remedy for assisting with withdrawal. Numerous clients have stopped smoking or drinking with CBD. By chance, smoking and drinking are one of the most widely recognized reasons for heart issues that can bring about genuine coronary illness

Hemp oil and solid rest

A solid rest influences our body as mental and physical wellness, reinforces the insusceptible framework, mental parity and adds to better organ and digestion capacities.

The most recent research demonstrates that around 33% of individuals experience the ill effects of rest issue. In the event that it's only a momentary issue, for example, a significant test, individual issues, thinking about an infant youngster, and so on., it shouldn't be dealt with restoratively. Be that as it may, if the rest unsettling influences keep going for quite a while, not by the human, yet in addition, its condition would already be able to see numerous undesirable reactions.

A sound rest influences our body as mental and physical wellness, reinforces the insusceptible framework, mental equalization and adds to better organ and digestion capacities. Individuals who experience the ill effects of rest issue, be it on account of pressure or on the off chance that it is a going with the manifestation of a malady, are progressively defenseless to different sicknesses.

Hemp oil as a tranq uilizer

Getting up in the first part of the day, being engaged, and dynamic and feeling great for the duration of the day is an unfulfilled want of numerous individuals. Albeit more youthful ages accept their absence of rest as a feature of their way of life, with expanding age, deficient and intruded on rest turns into a noteworthy issue. For this situation, numerous individuals resort to drugs that can, sadly, carry with them bothersome reactions (daytime tiredness, weariness, constrained responsiveness). Some rest meds might be recommended by the specialist just on a momentary premise since they can make the patient ward all-around rapidly.

Hemp oil is a simple common item (hemp concentrate is made with cold-squeezed hemp seed oil), thus far no logical research has called attention to its conceivable symptoms. CBD and different cannabinoids tie through the receptors to the endocannabinoid framework in our body and subsequently influence the nature of our rest. The ongoing examination has likewise affirmed that cannabinoids contained in hemp oil decrease torment and improve rest.

Rest issue is all the time a corresponding indication surprisingly who experience the ill effects of unending agony. Hence, it is prescribed to consider the admission of hemp oil. CBD hemp oil is likewise a viable tranquilizer in individuals experiencing uneasiness and stress-related rest issue.

Hemp oil and avoidance

To have the option to treat rest issue viably, one should initially get to the foundation of the causes. Hemp oil will be much progressively viable on the off chance that you continuously adjust your way of life well ordered to your resting propensities.

Here are a few hints:

- Pay regard for the utilization of espresso, liquor, and cigarettes (particularly toward the evening)

- Make sure your rest condition is free of aggravations

- Avoid drugs that can cause rest issue

- Exercise (in any event 3 times each week)

The battle to get thinner

Be that as it may, how does the CBD work as far as weight reduction?

The declaration that the CBD can help in this setting appears to be less natural. Could the picture of cannabis as a craving stimulant and sustenance hunger advertiser demonstrate the inverse? The appropriate response is no! The reason for craving coming about because of cannabis use is for the most part THC. Despite what might be expected, cannabidiol is regularly smothered, however that is not all:

Weight reduction through cannabidiol

This cannabinoid has an anorexia impact, diminishes hunger and anticipates craving. Also, individuals begin to positively affect the digestion and the consuming of fats. In what capacity would this be able to be clarified? A Korean report clarifies the subject and prompts the accompanying ends.

By animating qualities and proteins, oxidizing and degradable fats,

CBD positively affects digestion and encourages weight reduction.

CBD can build the number of mitochondria and increment their action.

CBD can repress proteins engaged with the creation of fat cells. On the off chance that their circulation is restricted, it likewise implies that the body gathers less fat.

Likewise, CBD can be utilized to treat tension and misery. For some individuals, these mental issue cause abundance nourishment and in this manner contribute altogether to overweight. Cannabidiol acts legitimately and in a roundabout way against weight. We trust it's a genuine recommendation.

Cannabis CBD in ADHD - option in contrast to drugs?

ADHD is a consideration shortage hyperactivity issue. Influenced endure somewhat enormous focus issues. Likewise, many still have hyperactive conduct. Possibly your youngsters are influenced or even you. You have effectively attempted numerous solutions for ADHD, however, none has made a difference? At that point, CBD in ADHD may be an answer that can work.

ADHD happens, particularly in youngsters and youths. Around five percent of all things considered and teenagers matured somewhere in the range of three and 17 years are said to be influenced. In some cases, this issue is taken into grown-up life since it doesn't simply vanish once more. In this way, it is very conceivable that it is seen distinctly in grown-ups. The treatment with cannabis stays intriguing.

CBD against ADHD?

The lack of ability to concentrate consistently issue, otherwise called ADHD or ADD, shows itself in various courses in influenced patients:

They are anything but difficult to occupy; they can't focus on their undertakings for quite a while and respond hastily over and over.

While ADD patients experience difficulty concentrating, ADHD patients are regularly extremely fretful and have the inclination to be consistently moving. This prompts the purported hyperactivity. Here, CBD ought to be viable in ADHD or CBD in ADHD.

Numerous individuals still accept that hyperactivity issue in kids and young people is the aftereffect of wrong instruction. Be that as it may, this isn't right, since it has been deductively demonstrated that this conduct issue is brought about by the absence of parity of significant delegate substances of the mind. These synapses are in charge of the greater part of the data handling in the mind. Most importantly, the envoy substance dopamine is available truth be told, all around marginally in individuals who have ADHD or ADD. Likewise, specialists have demonstrated that the cannabinoid receptor is additionally associated with the advancement of the confusion. Subsequently, it appears to be regular that CBD and ADHD some way or another have a place together in light of the fact that it can influence the body's framework, the supposed endocannabinoid framework.

How does cannabidiol work in ADHD?

A low focus and hyperactive conduct can be irritating in regular daily existence. Numerous individuals with ADHD are recommended Ritalin or comparable drugs, yet they can cause genuine reactions, for example, loss

Brad J. Simon

of hunger or dozing issues. CBD can be a decent option for ADHD.

This issue is otherwise called neurological brokenness. The cortisol level has risen while the dopamine level has diminished. This prompts an unevenness. CBD oil for ADHD should positively affect these two qualities. This, thusly, guarantees the indications can be diminished. CBD oil in ADHD has a major bit of leeway, on the grounds that there are for all intents and purposes no known symptoms, which is the reason you or your kids can without much of a stretch take it - obviously still at your own hazard and ideally simply after exhaustive research.

Is self-treatment conceivable in ADHD with cannabis?

With CBD for ADHD or CBD for ADHD self-treatment at your obligation is conceivable. In spite of the fact that the utilization of cannabis isn't identified with an improved capacity to focus, the inverse might be the situation.

Cannabis or CBD in ADHD - can the side

effects be mitigated?

In a US study, grown-ups who had ADD or ADHD were asked which side effects they are experiencing if cannabis isn't expended. Some experience the ill effects of consideration deficiency issue, others more from hyperactivity. Most importantly, the hyperactive practices ought to end up more grounded if nothing is taken. CBD oil is said to function admirably against ADHD and utmost hyperactivity - we have picked up that impression. Likewise, in young people, there were contemplates on how taking on the indications should influence. They were less confused and less hyperactive. The absence of fixation likewise diminished.

The oil can be a decent enhancement to the treatment

The old-style treatment of ADHD is separated into a few stages:

There are psychotherapeutic just as social helpful measures. Yet additionally, drugs are regulated. Principle speaking, medications, for example, Ritalin are utilized, which have an especially invigorating impact. They bolster the synapse capacity and increment focus, however numerous patients feel as though they are for all time invigorated.

Along these lines, CBD in ADHD can be a decent enhancement to diminish the indications, on the grounds that the experience on our part demonstrates that the alleviating, loosening up impact could be powerful here.

Perfect consideration for skin break out with CBD

Skin break out is a generally normal skin issue, which fundamentally happens during pubescence of a youngster, however at times maneuvers into adulthood. Discoveries from research appear, nonetheless, that cannabidiol could be a compelling common cure here. As a rule, skin issues can be dealt with very well with the dynamic substance from the cannabis plant and soothe manifestations.

What is skin break out?

Fortunately, skin breaks out isn't one of the most perilous sicknesses, regardless of whether it puts a great deal of strain on those influenced. For the most part, with her, constrained confidence, go up to disgrace and even mental issues. Sadly, skin break out is hard to conceal well, and even great make-up can't take out skin break out. Skin break out is a hormonal issue, which clarifies the expanded event during adolescence. The principal contact individual for skin break out is the dermatologist who frequently endorses unique drugs, which just assistance to a constrained degree.

In skin inflammation - and by the route additionally with unclean skin - the sebaceous organs are especially dynamic. Hormones transcendently control these and accommodate sebum creation and at last for oily skin. In the event that the hormones are in an irregularity, this can be perceived on the skin surface. Slight skin break out shows itself with individual pimples; solid skin breaks out methods an exceptionally solid sebum creation with practically full-inclusion stopped up sebaceous organs. The stopped up organs, in the long run, become aggravated, bringing about scarring and other incendiary procedures. The well-known pustules become bigger, and the whole skin falls apart.

Is it effectively utilizing CBD for skin break out?

Brad J. Simon

In the sebaceous organs and hair follicles, they have effectively found endocannabinoid receptors. These interface with the cannabinoid and follow up on simply those pieces of the skin. Since the sebaceous organs likewise cooperate with the body's cannabinoids, it is legitimate to expect that extra cannabinoids could enhance affect the skin's appearance. As per field reports, precisely this, hence a guideline of the sebaceous organ action, was affirmed.

Obviously, we definitely realize that CBD has a calming impact, which is likewise an issue with skin break out. Pimples are nothing else than aggravation inside the sebaceous organs. On the off chance that the mitigating CBD is utilized, the aggravation could be seriously constrained. Be that as it may, skin inflammation is and remains a side effect because of hormones. CBD is additionally ready to associate with the body's hormonal framework. In this way, CBD could be connected both inside and remotely for skin break out.

In light creams for the consideration of skin inflammation, frequently extra dynamic fixings are utilized, which bolster the skin recovery positive. So dynamic corrective fixings, for example, bisabolol (from fundamental chamomile oil), dexpanthenol, hyaluronic corrosive, aloe, and other uncommon plant concentrates are utilized, which keep the pores and sebaceous organs and give adequate dampness.

How would I use CBD for skin break out?

There are presently a few items available that could be taken or utilized in various ways. Above all else is the CBD oil, which depends on hemp oil. This oil can essentially be dribbled under the tongue so it very well may be consumed into the circulation system by means of the mucous films. In the body, it acts separately on the kindled territories and can control the hormonal irregularity. Thus, CBD is likewise utilized effectively during the menopause or menopause of a lady, in light of the fact that there are hormonal changes, prompting different indications.

Hyperactive oil organs produce a great deal of skin fat, and it generally returns to aggravation of the skin. The skin fat makes the skin sparkle considerably more with the goal that the skin inflammation seems much increasingly articulated. Simultaneously, the pores are stopped up; it comes to clog and clogged pores are framed. Any individual who pushes it further disturbs the circumstance by aggravating the tissue and causing scarring. A cycle that is hard to getaway.

In the meantime, there are likewise extraordinary CBD items, which can likewise be connected to the skin all things considered. For example, light recipes, which have been enhanced with extra common fixings, direct the pH of the skin. For this situation, CBD averts the irritation of the sebaceous organs from spreading and declining. The mitigating properties act legitimately on the skin; simultaneously, the skin is less oily.

Potential employments of CBD and skin break out

Skin break out creams or serums ought to be connected 2-3 times each day to purged skin. Whenever connected meagerly and uniformly, brilliant make-up can likewise be utilized.

Irritated, blushed skin is relieved.

Oily and sleek skin is directed.

Beautification of the skin.

Blemishes, for example, pimples, clogged pores, and skin inflammation pustules are less articulated.

The regular pH of the skin balances out.

To bolster skin recovery

Good items feed the skin, saturate it and furthermore help to avert untimely maturing of the skin.

CBD items are a characteristic option

without cortisone, arrangements are reasonable for long haul use.

The field of use of CBD is really adaptable, so it doesn't require clear skin break out to treat the skin with CBD.

Extra tip

Notwithstanding the fitting consideration, all things considered, the inside admission of CBD oil and exceptional micronutrients is additionally prescribed. The supplementation of zinc and pantothenic corrosive in the mix with an uncommon CBD Akneserum is especially powerful against flaws.

Conclusion

CBD represses lipid creation of skin cells and does not neutralize the physiological procedures of the skin. Accordingly, the skin isn't dried out and can standardize fat creation. All in all, it stays to be seen whether CBD will keep on common as a successful solution for flaws and skin break out. In any case, items with CBD can be bought lawfully, so sufferers like to fall back on the numerous positive encounters of skin break outpatients. In any case, researchers are now in understanding that CBD can be a promising medication in the battle against skin inflammation. Given, obviously, the self-treatment is upheld by adequate exercise, a ton of consideration and a sound eating regimen. Tragically, there are still no therapeutic items with CBD, however, it stays to be trusted.

CBD in despondency:

Provide help without reactions Cannabidiol (CBD) ought not just assistance with malignant growth, skin issues and diabetes yet in addition to emotional well-being issues, for example, tension, addictions or wretchedness. In this article, we take a gander at how CBD can help with sorrow. Numerous sufferers as of now swear by medicinal cannabis. In any case, what is the depressant impact dependent on?

Wretchedness:

The basic illness within recent memory

It is an illness with numerous manifestations, for example, gloom, an absence of positive emotions or a restrained drive. The vast majority feel discouraged at any rate once during their lifetime. Right around one out of five is influenced by genuine sorrow during their lifetime. On the off chance that the downturn keeps going longer or returns over and over, it can seriously confine the personal satisfaction of those influenced and even lead to self-destructive demise. The illness is along these lines in earnest need of treatment. A specialist ought to be counseled regardless. This is particularly obvious when self-destructive contemplations happen.

For the treatment of despondency

Brad J. Simon

Treatments or way of life changes frequently treats gloom. For the most part, drugs (antidepressants, MAO inhibitors, ketamine or specific reuptake inhibitors) are additionally utilized, yet they can have solid symptoms and may even compound misery. Run of the mill reactions of antidepressants incorporates rest issue, weight increase, and stomach inconvenience. They work straightforwardly in the cerebrum where they can rebalance the mind digestion that has left control. An ever-increasing number of patients are utilizing cannabinoids, for example, THC (tetrahydrocannabinol) or CBD (cannabidiol) to treat melancholy because of the many symptoms of antidepressants.

Data: CBD is viewed as to a great extent free of reactions. Just pregnant ladies should abstain from taking them to secure their kid. Those taking extra prescription should initially accommodate CBD consumption with the going to doctor on account of potential cooperations.

Therapeutic cannabis isn't a revelation however has been utilized for quite a long time, for instance, in parts of Europe and Asia. Patients report a state of mind improving impact through to elation at high dosages. Additionally, there is a quieting impact that happens, particularly in CBD. By chance, cannabinoids are not a solution for misery. Best case scenario they neutralize indications. CBD is utilized to fix the downturn; the activating elements must be dispensed with. Be that as it may, these are frequently previously and must be made do with treatment. Different triggers can be physical and should be dealt with as needs are. Consequently, irritation may likewise be in charge of despondency.

Therapeutic cannabis in misery: CBD or THC?

The shared characteristic of CBD and THC lies in their disposition improving impact. Both are fundamentally the same as concoction mixes of the cannabinoid type got from cannabis plants. In spite of the substance likeness, the two mixes cause incompletely various impacts. Likely the most noteworthy contrast lies in the psych movement, which briefly moves the individual worried to another condition of awareness. THC is psychoactive, while CBD isn't.

This property is synonymous with the "high-being". So THC causes a surge, while CBD does not require it. Incidentally, this implies it can likewise legitimately be bought and expended in many nations. Conversely, THC is illicit in numerous nations, with a functioning discussion on sanctioning right now occurring in Germany and different nations. Unexpectedly, shoppers of CBD are not pulled in by a clamor impact but rather carry on generally ordinary. We, in this way, prescribe you use CBD to decrease your downturn with cannabis. Any individual who experiences nervousness notwithstanding wretchedness should quit utilizing THC at any rate. Since rather than CBD, THC can build the uneasiness issue. CBD ought to likewise have the option to alleviate tension notwithstanding the state of mind improving impact.

The biochemical foundation of sadness and how cannabinoids influence

Our state of mind, our psychological prosperity and our whole character depend on biochemical procedures in our cerebrum. These procedures are constrained by envoy substances, for example, hormones and synapses, which must dock with appropriate receptors in the sensory system. Various assignments are additionally in charge of various hormones or synapses. On the off chance that the arrival of delivery people is aggravated for our prosperity or docking in the receptors, it might be in charge of melancholy. Cannabinoids can act straightforwardly on the control forms, accordingly decidedly impacting the sensory system lastly, the state of mind. This works either by managing the delivery of person substances or by tending to the receptors.

CBD in discouragement: extra impacts

Incidentally, if the reason for the downturn isn't an activating occasion yet is brought about by irritation, cannabidiol can help. Since the CBD compound improves the state of mind and alleviating as well as calming. Likewise, cancer prevention agents in cannabis make harmed cells simpler to fix and secure.

Brad J. Simon

Studies demonstrate the adequacy of cannabinoids in psychological instability

Studies affirm Cannabinoids soothingly affect sorrow. The stimulant impact of THC has been illustrated, for instance, in different creature tests. In concentrates that took a gander at the impact of THC on physical distress, it has been discovered that as a reaction, misery was additionally lightened by the cannabinoid. Comparable impacts were noted in concentrates on cannabis tranquilizes in the treatment of chemotherapy-related sickness and spewing. CBD is currently viewed as a quick-acting stimulant. Likewise, a US overview found that numerous individuals took cannabinoids predominantly for agony or emotional well-being issues, for example, discouragement and nervousness. Notwithstanding the investigations, there are incalculable positive tributes from fulfilled patients that can be gotten to on the Internet.

CBD can help who experiences melancholy and other psychological maladjustments

Fine.

Wretchedness is a genuine condition that can cause serious outcomes whenever left untreated. Therefore, a speedy treatment of the malady is firmly exhorted. Only one out of every odd patient needs to take antidepressants or different meds notwithstanding treatments. The issue: The most generally endorsed prescriptions have too solid symptoms. CBD and different cannabinoids are demonstrated to be successful in treating or assuaging melancholy through investigations and tributes from sufferers. There are just minor or no reactions. Pregnant ladies should look for an option to cannabinoids to ensure the tyke. On the off chance that you are as of now taking prescription normally, you should initially talk about the utilization of CBD with the specialist due to potential connections.

Does expending CBD lead to a positive medication test?

Each cannabis purchaser, at some point or another, stresses over what happens when a medication test is expected. Furthermore, exactly with regards to driver's permit, many begin perspiring. Generally, be that as it may, such a test is possibly made if there is doubt of medication misuse. What's more, since CBD is certainly not a psychoactive substance that causes certain variations from the norm, for example, red-eye, there is no compelling reason to stress over the police directing a medication test during an ordinary traffic control. In any case, you ought to be set up for it, on the off chance that it ends up like that.

What sorts of medication test are there?

As the name infers, the medication test serves to give proof of whether certain breakdown results of medications or medications are found in an individual's body. What's more, to test that, there are various techniques:

Pee Test:

When in doubt, these are test strips, which are plunged in the still warm pee, which the suspect has recently given. After just a couple of minutes, the outcome ends up obvious. This sort of test is one of the most solid and instructive on the grounds that even following a few days or weeks (contingent upon which substance was devoured), corruption items can at present be identified. In any case, it ought to be noticed that even the aloof inward breath of cannabis can prompt a positive test.

Hair test:

The hair examination is especially dreaded. Since a hair test can demonstrate medication use, which is as of now quite a while prior. For instance, in an individual with a hair length of 40 cm, it is conceivable to demonstrate utilization that was at that point 4 years back. When all is said in done, one just looks at whether medications have been utilized in the previous a half year. Different substances and their metabolites are saved in the hair, which remains in or on the body with the hair.

Blood gathering:

The blood is taken when doubt has been affirmed by a quick medication test (pee or wipe test). For the most part to decide whether the suspect is affected by medications. Furthermore, contingent upon what was devoured, the substances are perceptible in the blood somewhere in the range of 1 and 48 hours. For the most part, be that as it may, it as of now needs an unmistakable and reasonable doubt or different history to have the option to play out a blood test.

Drug wipe test:

This fast test is likewise done all the time in light of the fact that the subject gets no opportunity to control the outcome. For this reason, a perspiration or spit test is taken with a test strip. These antibodies on it respond with those present in the perspiration or spit antibodies and along these lines lead to the shading change of the test strip.

The contrast between CBD and THC

Frequently it happens that the two substances are crossed by obliviousness, some of the time even by the authorities themselves. Shoppers, obviously, know the genuine contrasts and impacts on the body. They likewise comprehend what impact the separate substances have on the body.

THC

Tetrahydrocannabinol, THC is a cannabinoid gotten from the hemp plant, which has a psychoactive impact. Especially wealthy in THC are the pollinated blossoms of the female Sativa plant, which have around 6 to 20% of cannabinoids. The seeds, thusly, contain no THC and can in this manner additionally be purchased and expended decisively, as long as the seed isn't utilized for development. THC is prevalent for both medicinal and recreational use

Up until this point, we realize that THC follows up on two receptors with assurance. Since it collaborates with our endocannabinoid framework in the body and its CB1 and CB2 receptors, these are principally situated in our focal sensory system, where they direct the arrival of synapses.

The impact changes from individual to individual, obviously, however when all is said in done, it takes around 2-3 hours. Also, these are the most widely recognized impacts of the substance:

You feel genuinely loose and feel a euphoric impact, which means "high".

Brad J. Simon

Different perspectives open up and the typical examples of reasoning lose their significance.

Observation changes, time passes all the more gradually, minor things are seen on the double. The body feeling is simpler. Then again, in any case, so loosened up that each development is slower.

It is simpler to understand others, and social conduct with individual customers is seen as increasingly extreme and fun. The momentary memory endures a bit during the inebriation. It isn't extraordinary for buyers to begin a sentence and sever it midway since they never again realize what they are after.

Be that as it may, it might likewise come to not all that lovely inebriation, when THC overdoses or the body/mind does not adapt to the inebriation:

The considerations can overpower you on the grounds that there is an excessive number of who are attempting to pass on something confusedly and wildly.

Film breaks can happen in light of the fact that transient memory is weakened.

Circulatory issues, quick tachycardia, sickness can be the outcome if a lot of is expended.

It might likewise happen that somebody in the wake of devouring no more want felt social to make a move, however, would prefer to be distant from everyone else for themselves.

Individuals with psychological wellness issues could be exacerbated in their negative considerations. While utilizing CBD may help with fits of anxiety and tension, THC may increment or trigger it.

Reactions when utilizing cannabis are not known and must be ascribed to different individual reports. In the event that you don't feel well and for the most part don't have an uplifting demeanor towards utilization, you won't discover the impact extraordinary either.

CBD

CBD and THC, from one perspective, the two cannabinoids supplement each other consummately, and on the other, they have their disparities. CBD is likewise a cannabinoid of the hemp plant and is considered non-psychoactive. Whereby it positively affects the body. CBD is as yet considered the restorative supernatural occurrence weapon of cannabinoids second to none. Since utilization does not influence the shopper, as in he is "high" or "stoned" skimming on cloud 7.

CBD communicates with the CB1 and CB2 receptors in our endocannabinoid framework, killing the impacts of THC while hindering tension or distress. Thus it influences the body:

Not psychoactive

Soothing and quieting for the body

The muscles unwind

many restorative angles

Conceivable symptoms can be:

- May hinder hepatic medication digestion.

- Dry mouth

- dizziness

- fatigue

- Increased tremor in Parkinson's (with inaccurate measurements)

Low circulatory strain

In any case, once more, the facts demonstrate that there are conceivable reactions that infrequently, if not happen. The unadulterated CBD is 100% lawful in Germany and can be uninhibitedly sold and acquired. Nonetheless, it is essential to guarantee that solitary a THC substance of 0.2% or less might be available.

Impact on the medication test

To answer the effect on a medication test in the wake of expending CBD, the various methods of activity ought to be clear. Who smokes cannabis or generally expends THC, which will get a positive test in the hands. The utilization of CBD oil or different arrangements in which just CBD was removed, does not prompt a positive test outcome.

At the point when a medication test is done, it is typically looked for THC and its significant metabolite 11-nor-9-carboxy-Δ9 (THC-COOH). CBD itself is normally not tried by any means, as it's anything but a medication even in police circles. Be that as it may, it is accounted for that there have been sure test outcomes despite the fact that the shopper was uniquely in contact with CBD arrangements.

Moreover, it ought to be noticed that CBD is gotten among others from the hemp plant assortment Sativa, which contains large amounts of THC. So it might happen that particularly with modernly fabricated CBD items, regularly hints of it very well may be found. Utilization enduring half a month and high measurement leave different follows, which obviously were not seen by the customer.

A test with 15 members has just been led on this point. Subjects who got CBD oil with a THC substance of 0.09 mg to 0.6 mg were tried positive utilizing a pee test, radioimmunoassay and gas chromatographic-mass spectrometry. Nonetheless, it was found from the test that no individual with a portion of 0.45 mg THC had surpassed the farthest point of 50 mg/ml.

It might well happen that the utilization of enormous amounts of cannabinoid can prompt a positive medication test, regardless of whether modest quantities of THC are contained in that. Also, to forestall that, exacting self-guideline of measurement is an absolute necessity. The items utilized ought to be all around inquired about, or more all, it ought to be clear what precisely is inside.

Another little tip: THC is generally noticeable somewhere in the range of 4 and 12 days. Contingent upon your physical condition, wellness, diet, a measure of utilization and digestion. The more and the more it has been devoured, the more it can normally be demonstrated.

Rights after utilization of CBD

The standard police quick tests are, obviously, deliberate and could be denied. Be that as it may, to what degree this bodes well, everybody needs to choose for themselves. In the event that there is a doubt of medication maltreatment with respect to the police, the test ends up mandatory. These incorporate the smell of medications, a rising apprehension, and an obvious driving style. Indeed, even expanded students or other atypical body sign can give the police the privilege to play out a brisk medication test. Also, not just that, a

Brad J. Simon

blood test would then be able to be on solicitation in the room if the accomplishment of the examination ought to be in threat (§ 81a passage 2 Stops). In any case, regardless of whether a judge must be called or not, fluctuates from state to state. Be that as it may, in this nation, the privilege to not effectively take an interest in its exchange applies. The pee test shows the utilization of sedatives, cannabis, cocaine, methamphetamine, heroin, happiness (MDMA, MDE, MDA) and amphetamines. In a negative test, the buyer has nothing to fear. Whenever assessed decidedly, be that as it may, the pee test can be a purpose behind a legitimately permitted blood test. This, thus, is considered as proof in court and is consequently so dreaded.

When can the blood test be performed?

By and large, it requires a positive pee test ahead of time, which as of now recommends that his offense was submitted. On the off chance that the pee test ends up being negative, at that point typically, no blood test might be done, just certainly. On the off chance that the pee test is denied regardless of an irrefutable doubt, the blood test can be constrained.

Cannabis wound up legitimate, the industry wherein it was made kept on developing. Legislators are presently battling for a stage for approval of absolute weed since this disposition is so famous and it appears the neighborhood message each week is a homeland that has turned into the objective of the creation and clearance of nourishment. In suburbia, organizations need to grow their showcasing endeavors.

That is very troublesome. Google isn't especially inspired by noticeable web indexes, particularly on their site, to advance pot items, in spite of the fact that the laws that they have made are legitimate. Makers needed to discover different approaches to sell their items.

Regardless of this street bar, the cannabis item blast occurred because of the blast of stick fame during this decade. Since THC and CBD can enter the body from numerous points of view - smoking, gulping, gulping, skin contact - the number of items made with it isn't rare, obviously, bounty. A few items, notwithstanding, appear to be notable or if nothing else develops.

Brad J. Simon

Note that this article does not comprise proposals for one of the referenced items. Since Canada is as yet illicit at the government level and delegated the 1 tangle in the rundown, the measure of research it works is constrained. This state is only a tribute to mainstream sorts of items, where Cannabis is lawfully legitimate.

1. Canvas oil

Obviously, it is a genuinely general class in itself. There are weed items containing cannabidiol oil (CBD) to accomplish the ideal impact. In any case, cannabis oils in various sizes can be taken. This adaptability is effectively the most looked for after for the individuals who need to utilize lawful Canada items.

CBD oils contain not very many THC substances, so you don't typically connect the most extreme level with pot. Along these lines, you can accomplish conceivably wanted impacts - help with discomfort, uneasiness alleviation, queasiness, and so on - without the mental reaction.

Epilepsy is where the utilization of cannabis oil is reliably bolstered at the government level. The US

Food and Drug Administration (FDA) has consistently endorsed its Federal Advisory Committee with the goal that a pharmaceutical physicist known as epidote can be affirmed, which can be utilized for the treatment of some uncommon epilepsy. CBD oil has likewise been valuable in relief from discomfort, disease treatment, tension, misery and rest issue, among others.

CBD oils may exist as a different utility unit, and it offers different alternatives for browsing huge organizations to be made and sold. The most widely recognized type of e-fluid for a vape pen is another ticker. CBD parts fall under your tongue and are as often as possible retained into the scribed concentrate and mouth. There are containers that can be taken with water as a customary pill.

Obviously, on the off chance that anybody needs legitimate cannabis oil, the representative does not need it, he keeps the CBD oil in his tongue and melts it. A few drug stores in the CBD refrigerator oil are sold legitimately.

2. Cannabis excellence items and healthy skin items

Brad J. Simon

As the development of CBD and expanded legitimization of cannabis in more nations, a few organizations and business people have concocted showcasing these items, who regularly don't sell weeds: subsequently, the CBD excellence items industry is developing quickly consistently - despite the fact that it isn't utilized by provincial ladies as it were.

Aside from the above advantages, CBD likewise has fiery properties because of cannabis receptors on the skin. A few analysts state that it is circled to build the torment, hydration, or even liberality in skin inflammation and cannabis excellence/healthy skin items.

A large number of these items are centered around CBD and the medical advantages it gives. In any case, there are likewise more THCs; dispensaries are accessible.

3. Cannabis drinks

Cannabis beverages don't arrive at the standard statures of magnificence, however, they are increasingly open. Malignant growth-filled mixed drinks are still in their youth, generally setting off to certain bars in Los Angeles, yet recreational marijuana use is legitimate in more states, however, it is a pattern that can develop quickly.

Yet, the main beverage that is given for CBD test is a lager. Since, aside from all the past impacts of cannabinoids, the cannabis supplies various sums and flavors. There are a few streets along the street, predominantly due to the US Statement and Schedule 1 isn't one of the meds. Notwithstanding, the arrangement has been fathomed, particularly for distilleries and bottling works that live in states with lawful weeds.

4. Cannabis chocolate

Nourishment is particularly prevalent in light of the fact that they are more probable than different techniques. It currently allows you to nibble while taking your legitimate drug, which is or more. The most outstanding edibles are the most widely recognized criteria - weed dark-colored, hotcake and Maryjane tough (which once in a while kids inadvertently oversee issues identified with nervousness concerns).

Since it wound up legitimate, and organizations need to keep cannabis items in the market, they are such chocolate that has moved toward becoming something of the pattern. Chocolate can be offered to the individuals who are keen on going after for lawful weed, however, the individuals who need increasingly "advanced" strategies than to smoke together. It gives organizations a chance to attempt a more modern showcasing effort than what they call a sticky bear.

These chocolates are sold in a constrained manner, typically in light of the fact that they contain THC

5. Cannabis Gummies

Treat you need, yet not chocolate? There is no worry. Gammy, particularly CBD-explicit, ended up one of the most prevalent items subsequent to being substantial Maryjane. Albeit still in a sporadic zone, which means it is hard to decide the amount CBD it has, it is presently very pointless to see CBD gamma packs in nearby service stations are not abnormal.

On the off chance that you live in a nation with therapeutic Maryjane and have a medicinal pot card (or living in a nation, including legitimate beguilement marina and have arrived at lawful age), your nearby drug store is certain to pick gum brew, bugs and more for you. Regardless of whether it is with CBD or THC Green Rhodes and Diamond CBD organizations are weeds, where they offer numerous CBD games for them. Gummer is one of the most widely recognized choices accessible for individuals searching for something scrumptious effectively.

6. Cannabis containers

Not as sweet or as reviving as lager, chocolate and gum, containers are a possibility for them that simply need to accomplish something for the reason. Cases are progressively prevalent for them who are not searching for a nibble with their weeds and rather accept it as medications - this is the thing that numerous individuals in the nation accomplish for it.

Cases are frequently the most prevalent for utilizing CBDs. For instance, the Medicine Man referenced in Colorado sells both CBD containers and cannabin

Brad J. Simon

(CBN) cases. It might be as simple as searching for different containers of roses.

How might I dispose of my body's THC, maybe because of a cannabis detox?

Canvas Detox: Unfortunately, THC is in the body longer than numerous different substances. There are numerous reasons that you need to get THC quicker in your body. Much of the time, in any case, you can check for drugs, and you likely would prefer not to draw consideration.

All in all, what is the quickest method to THC launch from the body?

Sadly, there is no "Panacea" to discharge the body from THC. In the event that there is one and the staying in protected mode, pause and repel cannabis from you! In any case, you definitely realize that.

Here are the normal scores that can be followed in standard score thinks about:

- Blood: 1 to 7 days

- Hair: 90 days

- Saliva: 1 to 7 days

A few components/changes invest energy disposing of THC:

Your digestion

How regularly are the weeds eaten

Physical Mass Index (BMI) (The higher the number, it takes)

How incredible it is to eat cannabis

How much cannabis is utilized?

No medications are analyzed

Cancer detox genuine business!

Each body reacts diversely to detoxification strategies. It is significant that you hear your body and don't acknowledge it! Utilize just normal solutions for such a detox. It doesn't damage to see your PCP. When all is said in done, I will just utilize this technique in a total crisis.

1. Detox drinks

Brad J. Simon

Most likely the least demanding approach to rapidly finish a medication assessment. Detox beverages are exceptionally prevalent in any case! On a fundamental level, the pee ought to be weakened here and in this manner take out the irritating THC from the body! Begin with this strategy as ahead of schedule as possible. Normally, 1-3 days are sufficient.

There are detox drinks that are compelling, and others are definitely not. Everyone responds contrastingly to such beverages, however, they are not hurtful! It might be that you have to visit the bathroom somewhat more frequently with these beverages.

2. On the off chance that you have one more week to go to medication testing, at that point the game is perhaps the best choice. Through the game, you can dispense with the total THC from your body! There is a little BUT ... As referenced above, THC is put away in fat cells, so there is a hazard that gets over into your circulatory system through the Sport THC. Ensure you don't do sports 24 hours before the medication test! Or on the other hand, you endeavor hard. This technique

is still viable on the off chance that you pursue the standards!

3. Sauna

Goodness, loosening up a bit consistently functions admirably, isn't that so? In a matter of seconds before your medication test, you should rapidly keep running into a sauna. THC can be identified in perspiration. What's more, there a sauna enables very well for cannabis to detox.

An investigation found that cops who came into contact with methamphetamine and different medications have extraordinarily helped sauna visits to get these substances off their bodies.

Along these lines, rapidly to the sauna, possibly there is something for the faculties.

4. Weakening

Weakening sounds interesting from the outset. Be that as it may, on the off chance that you realize that you need to complete a pee test, drink as much as you can! This technique isn't truly dependable, yet in a tough situation, the fallen angel eats flies. At that point, you should see that you drink as much as you can. Be that as it may, don't overstate! Tune in to your body.

5. A sound eating regimen

That implies products of the soil day by day in colossal amounts! In all honesty, however, most THC, you can "poo out" (pardon my words). Begin with your eating regimen in any event 3 days before the medication test.

The foods are grown from the ground help you to animate your assimilation. Also, the more you need to go to the washroom, the better it will be for you and your future medication test. The contained micronutrients can likewise enable your cannabis to detox.

These things can likewise help in your eating regimen: B nutrients (particularly niacin), initiated carbon (just if the THC is still in your stomach related tract, after hash brownies for instance) and magnesium.

CHAPTER :-2

METHODS OF USAGE AND WHAT TO USE IT FOR

Tincture Consumption

CBD Tinctures:

Everything you have to know Most CBD-based items are so new to them are accessible for a couple of years or less, which is the reason we, for the most part, don't have much data about them. Much of the time, it even appears to be simpler to discover the items themselves than to get exact data about them. Today we are examining another and top of the line item, tinctures from the CBD.

What are clean tinters?

A CBD tincture is a fluid nourishment supplement with an exceptionally high substance of cannabidiol. Make tinctures by dousing the CBD-rich hemp blooms in a high level of liquor and cooking on low warmth for a few hours. You can likewise utilize vinegar or glycerin rather than liquor, at the end of the day, liquor creates the best tinctures. The procedure requires some investment, however, is extremely straightforward.

When the fluid is prepared, it is normally blended with a sweet-tasting bearer oil, for instance, of orange or peppermint. The main tincture can be unpleasant. The last item ought to be viable with high CBD and close to 0.3% THC (tetrahydrocannabinol). When shopping, recollect that the CBD tincture is altogether different from the tincture of cannabis containing all cannabinoids, including THC. What's more, the CBD tincture isn't psychoactive, which means you won't get high.

Step by step instructions to USE Tinctures

Since tinctures are concentrated, they should just be taken in little portions. Most items arrive in a container with a dropper, and a few clients use pipettes. Overdose does not result in overdose or something like that, and huge dosages are pointless for most CBD remedial clients. If despite everything you need to portion higher, take a couple of more drops.

Numerous patients stress over the harsh taste, so they blend their tinctures with nourishment and drinks. The vast majority of the tincture comprises of soups, a plate of mixed greens dressings, espresso, and tea. Different clients take them sublingually, for example under the language. Studies have demonstrated that substances that are taken sublingually are retained quicker by the body than other oral strategies.

On the off chance that you sublingually take CBD tincture, you should ensure that the tincture stays under the tongue for at any rate one moment so it very well may be retained before ingestion of the rest. The sub-tongue layer enables you to be ingested through the sublingual course. From that point, the tincture, at last, arrives at the cerebrum through the outside carotid course and afterward through the interior carotid corridor. After around 15 minutes, the impacts can begin.

WHAT ARE THE ADVANTAGES?

CBD Tinctures can be utilized to supplement anything you might want to supplement with typical CBD oil. Since the tincture is concentrated, you just need to take a little portion for similar impacts. CBD by and large and tinctures, specifically, can be utilized to keep up a solid way of life and treat different illnesses - even though you ought to consistently counsel a specialist.

For instance, you can take them cautiously for the day as they needn't bother with the arrangement and don't should be steamed or steamed. The exemplifying containers themselves are extremely little and simple to cover up in a satchel or pack. The high tincture focus gives agreeable admission. Since just limited quantities are required, you can without much of a stretch modify your everyday portion with supreme exactness.

How to Use CBD - Complete Guide?

What is the best strategy for utilizing CBD? All rely upon you. Our items are utilized as oils, tinctures, copying oils, sublingual splashes, nourishments, and creams for topical application. What is the best utilization of CBD?

The best technique relies upon your inclination and the ideal impact. For instance, an individual with joint pain agony would like to apply a topical cream to the joints to facilitate the torment. There is nothing amiss with utilizing another technique. Which one you lean toward depends totally on the ideal portion and length of activity.

Consequently, there is no compelling reason to give CBD oil. Ensure that cannabinoids enter your body and give you the ideal impact. Most CBD clients incline toward sustenances or colors on account of the last more. Inward breath might be ideal for lightening distress in minutes. For this situation, in any case, the impact does not keep going for such a long time. 2 Also, remember that you are not constrained to one strategy! A few people utilize the choice in the first part of the day and one night. For instance, a few people expend nourishment toward the beginning of the day or use stains and smoke at night. The favored technique, subsequently, relies upon the ideal method of activity and length.

These four techniq ues are most reasonable for applying CBD

There are four fundamental approaches to expend CBD: oral, topical, sublingual, and by inward breath. In any case, there is something critical to note with regards to expending CBD. The particular impact of the picked technique for application may fluctuate from individual to individual. The impact is along these lines all around prone to differ from individual to person. Indeed, even with a similar application strategy, the impacts can be unique. Likewise, a few components influence the experience of the client.

The techniques referenced above of utilizing CBD have roused the improvement of different items and whole product offerings. For instance, vaporization has turned out to be progressively prominent as of late, especially as a result of the likelihood of prudently expending CBD openly or outside your very own

Brad J. Simon

home. Vaporization is likewise one of the best techniques for application. The substance is warmed to a specific temperature without consuming, similar to the case with smoking. Clients of this technique can, along these lines, devour an assortment of cannabinoids, terpenes, and flavonoids. These substances have their belongings other than the helpful impacts of cannabis and CBD.

Even though breathing in vapors is perhaps the most ideal approaches to devour CBD, a few people like to take CBD orally. Nourishments, for example, cannabis-included sustenances or beverages, cases, pills, and different tablets are extraordinary for taking. CBD oil alone has an abnormal taste that might be unreasonably solid for certain individuals.

Taking CBD else, it might be progressively valuable for certain individuals. In any case, it ought to be noticed that the impact of oral CBD is ordinarily 30 to an hour.

The impact of orally managed CBD may keep going for four hours or more. Contrasted with breathing in with a vape-pen or other vaporization gadget, the impacts are slower.

CBD - Topical application

Another significant utilization of CBD is a topical application. These incorporate items, for example, salves containing CBD, treatments, creams, and oils. The topical application results of CBD are one of a kind from numerous points of view. One of the principle purposes behind this is the client does not feel high during or after the application. Individuals that experience the ill effects of interminable torment of any sort, illness, or ailment can profit by items for topical use.

A significant motivation behind why CBD is frequently topically connected is the concentrated and quick pain-relieving impact experienced by clients. Topical CBD items are the best topical analgesics. They can be connected to various pieces of the body.

Less notable is that topical CBD items contain other dynamic cannabinoids that are consumed by the body through the skin. The cannabinoids join to the skin's CB2 receptors, actuating the body's endocannabinoid framework.

Brad J. Simon

Items for topical utilization of CBD are one of the most well-known techniques for application since they give help and unwinding without releasing the client high or restricting the psyche. Likewise, torment diminishing salves, moisturizers, or creams with CBD can be connected whenever, anyplace, without constraining regular exercises.

CBD - Sublingual Administration

Another significant technique for the utilization of CBD is sublingual organization, in which the sublingual items are set in the mouth and put under the tongue. The veins in the mouth assimilate the particular cannabinoids contained in the item. A few instances of sublingual CBD items are dissolvable strips, sublingual showers, tinctures, and tablets.

When all is said in done, the sublingual organization of CBD is perhaps the best strategy for the organization. The elements of these items are ingested through the oral mucosa, which is perfect for grabbing an assortment of cannabinoids. The sublingual organization of CBD offers clients a practically quick impact. In a sublingual organization, the dynamic substances are preferred ingested over different strategies.

All things considered, there are a few phenomenal CBD application strategies for individuals from everywhere throughout the world. Regardless of why CBD is expended, there is a technique that fits the individual needs and inclinations of the client. Ahead of time, you ought to be altogether educated, attempt diverse application strategies, and after that figure out which works best.

CBD Dosage: How Much Should You Take?

of CBD invested individuals has expanded significantly, particularly lately. When you have settled on the correct items, nearly everybody is gotten some information about the right portion of CBD. What number of drops do you have to take cannabinoid oil? What is incorporated into CBD?

4 short tips for right CBD oil dose

There are numerous measurements proposals for the CBD on the web, however, they are some of the time truly flawed. All in all, it tends to be said that one should best focus on understanding and ought to counsel a specialist is fundamental.

Tip 1: Start a little!

Learners should begin with a moderately little portion. Thusly, you can gradually work your way through something and not hazard taking "to an extreme" when required. This applies to both the CBD content and the quantity of day by day drops/cases, and so on.! It is accepted that a few drops of a 10% CBD oil are utilized two times every day.

Tip 2: just increment the portion gradually!

To evaluate whether the current CBD portion is directly for you, you should take a similar sum for a few days and afterward attempt a higher portion if essential.

Tip 3: Take a little advances!

As in Tip 1, it is additionally significant not to abuse. Thusly, it is suggested that you move in little amounts when dosing cannabidiol items.

Tip 4: if there should be an occurrence of issues, the specialist makes a difference

In the event that somebody has issues or vulnerabilities in deciding the ideal sum, the mindful specialist can deal with the circumstance

WHAT IS THE PERFECT MEASURE OF CBD?

CBD oil is an individual on the grounds that every creature responds in an unexpected way. In this manner, it is hard to give proposals for dose. For instance, a couple of drops of a 5 percent CBD oil could as of now influence one human while another ten drops would be required.

For another situation, 3 drops of 2% oil could work. Subsequently, it is frequently prescribed, to begin with, a 2-or 5-percent CBD low-portion oil and store it for a couple of days. In the event that no impact happens, the portion might be expanded.

Likewise, producers, for the most part, give a dose proposal that is typically low with undesirable symptoms. This does not imply that consequently, everybody ought to pick a higher dose. As referenced before, you should begin with a low portion and gradually increment the portion on the off chance that you don't feel it following a couple of days.

Measurements proposals from studies

Studies covering just a cannabidiol portion appropriate for the standard client are not yet accessible. The particular CBD portions were individual in the rest of the investigations - cannabidiol was commonly utilized in the accessible human examinations in specific maladies, for example, epilepsy, Parkinson's ailment, or schizophrenia. The dosages differ enormously relying upon the condition and seriousness.

Summing up a few investigations, grown-ups who experience the ill effects of CBD take 100-800 mg of cannabidiol. In youngsters, various dosages of 2 to 25 mg/kg body weight were utilized. Reactions were 25 mg/kg body weight - incredibly high portions are presumably not required. A 30 kg kid would need to take 750 mg of cannabidiol day by day - that is practical, and as a rule, lower dosages have demonstrated powerful. Experience has demonstrated that overdose can scarcely be accomplished or not in any way.

On the off chance that you experience the ill effects of nervousness issue, focuses beneath 50 mg are as of now compelling, despite the fact that the force of the indications is probably going to assume a job here.

Proposals of the makers of CBD oils

One drop for the correct measurements of cannabidiol.

This measurement is by all accounts extremely low - from one perspective, such little amounts could as of now be successful relying upon the field of utilization, then again, the makers might likewise want to fence. The suggested admission is low on any dietary enhancement bundling to shield it from undesirable symptoms.

Is there a danger of overdose?

The inquiry "What number of drops of CBD oil should I take?" On the one hand, it is to a great extent insufficient to take on the other and the dread of overdose.

Up until this point, there is no sign that reactions happen even at high measurements of the oil.

How to portion CBD oil?

There are measurements suggestions for CBD oil, which by and large shift somewhere in the range of 5 and 200 mg. The dose of CBD oil is reliant on various factors and the clinical image of every individual. One drop of CBD oil contains somewhere in the range of 0.7 and 6.5 mg cannabidiol.

A decent begin for the measurement is 5 mg CBD. This generally compares to:

- 4 drops of the 5% CBD oil

- 2 drops of 10% CBD oil

Cannabidiol (CBD) isn't a segment of a pharmaceutical medication however a characteristic cure. In any case, the extent of CBD is wide and ranges from genuine ailments to mellow torment. It might be all the more strengthening or quieting relying upon the measurements.

The investigations so far utilized sums somewhere in the range of 5 and 1,500 mg CBD every day. The focal point of the examinations so far has been on genuine ailments, for example, epilepsy, Crohn's malady, Parkinson's infection, constant torment, or schizophrenia.

Endless reports demonstrate that CBD oil likewise affects wellbeing cognizant however not sick individuals. There are still just a couple of logical examinations on the precise measurements proposal for regular day to day existence.

Before we begin with the most significant data is quickly referenced that there is still no panacea for the measurements (more subtleties later in the content). Everybody should test for themselves where the correct portion is.

Brad J. Simon
Nuts and bolts of dosing of CBD oil

Principally, it is imperative to know how much milligrams of cannabidiol is in a drop of oil. This relies upon the size of the bead, the blending proportion to the transporter oil, and the CBD focus. The definite sum may shift somewhat for the various producers and the above criteria.

What amount cannabidiol is in a drop of CBD oil?

- 5% ≈ 1.6 mg
- 10% ≈ 3.2 mg
- 15% ≈ 5 mg
- 20% ≈ 6.5 mg

A 10 ml container relates to around 300 drops. The accurate subtleties are more often than (not generally) on the sites of the maker to discover.

If you don't mind note: in the event that you take two drops of the 5% or one drop of the 10% CBD oil, you will get the equivalent. In the two cases, you take about

3.2 mg cannabidiol to you. The provided measure of CBD is the equivalent conveyed uniquely on 2 drops.

5 hints for the right dose of CBD oil

1. Begin little with the CBD dose

In the event that you are simply beginning to take CBD oil, at that point it is prescribed, to begin with, a little portion and gradually increment it until the ideal impact happens. A decent beginning portion is around 2-3 mg CBD. That would mean 2 drops of 5% CBD oil.

2. Gradually increment the portion

Begins with one drop (CBD 5%) in the first part of the day and one drop at night. Inevitably, increment as required by one drop each in the first part of the day and the night.

This methodology takes into consideration a steady way to deal with the perfect portion. Gradually you get an inclination for taking the oil and its belongings. Along these lines, you figure out how to portion it effectively relying upon the territory of use and use it at the ideal time.

3. Test a similar measure of CBD more than a few days

Stays at a similar point and don't build the portion each day. Give yourself and your body time to change in accordance with the measurement. Maybe a further increment isn't vital in light of the fact that your body just takes somewhat longer to deal with the cure.

4. CBD Dosage - Do not try too hard

When taking CBD, more isn't really more. It likely could be that a too high portion brings no further beneficial outcome.

Then again, frequently just an expanded portion prompts the ideal impact. For extreme inconvenience or agony, I would twofold or triple the typical portion. CBD oil is certifiably not a risky medication and has few reactions. Just collaborations with different medications ought to be considered.

5. Locate the correct brand for you

The nature of the oils in the market differs and with it, the impact of the separate item. As per a recent report led by Canna, one must not generally confide in the maker's data. Some bogus data has been found on the CBD substance of the oils. Illuminate yourself, construct trust, and feel good with your choice.

Full concentrates with an expansive range of dynamic fixings (CBD, CBDA, CBG, THC, terpenes, flavonoids) are desirable over CBD confines. The nature of the oils decides the impact and ought not to be thought little of. In another article, we have featured the subject of CBD oil quality in incredible detail.

Bit of leeway of CBD oil

One of the tremendous advantages of CBD oil is its adaptability in administering. Why? Tormentor strain is typically surprising and all of a sudden. With CBD oil, you can respond to it at short notice and as required.

CBD oil - measurements suggestion from the maker

Most makers give a measurement proposal or the greatest prescribed everyday portion. The prescribed day by day portion as a rule changes somewhere in the range of 2 and 30 mg CBD. The information for the most extreme everyday portion is somewhere close to 50 and 100 mg.

We have discovered that a 5% CBD oil from a producer An is regularly not equivalent to the oil of a similar convergence of a maker B. The nature of the oil normally influences its impact and subsequently likewise on the dose. In the event that the supplier transforms, it might likewise be important to reset the dose. For our situation, we had the option to bring down the portion to some degree because of the higher quality.

The nature of the oil relies upon the one hand on the nature of the crude materials utilized, I., and e. The hemp plant itself, and on the other on the handling, I., e. The assembling procedure.

CBD oil dosing help

Finding the correct measurements may not appear to be so natural from the outset. We looked through examinations, sites, and YouTube and asked actually from makers. But then it is hard to give an exact measurement proposal. Just the correct measurement can be found independent of anyone else. All things considered, there are a couple of harsh rules that have risen up out of a gathering of proposals.

CBD oil - torment measurement by body weight

Obviously, bodyweight assumes a job, and as of now referenced, it is imperative to become acclimated to these qualities. The accompanying table gives the prescribed admission relying upon the seriousness of the torment.

	MASS					
	< 10 kg	10-20 kg	20-40 kg	40-70 kg	70-100 kg	> 100 kg
PAIN						
Light	4.5 mg	6 mg	9 mg	12 mg	18 mg	20 mg
medium	6 mg	9 mg	12 mg	15 mg	20 mg	30 mg
Heavy	9 mg	12 mg	15 mg	18 mg	27 mg	45 mg

CBD overdose - Can I take an excessive amount of cannabidiol?

Since cannabidiol (CBD) is utilized by numerous clients to help battle illness and its side effects, a few items are considered by some to be practically medicinal. Along these lines, the client may pose the inquiry: Can I take an excessive amount of CBD? Is there an overdose or an overdose of cannabidiol? Does an excessive amount of sum cause reactions?

CBD overdose - begin little!

The subject of an overdose of CBD at first prompts the dose method. This ought to be finished relying upon the individual concerned and the proposed impact. Specifically, the proportion of CBD and the psychoactive operator THC is deciding. It ought to be noticed that legitimate items in Germany may just have a most extreme THC substance of 0.2% and subsequently don't cause an inebriating, psychoactive impact.

When all is said in done, the measurement of CBD, be that as it may, is that it ought to be moderately little toward the start and after that gradually expanded. Along these lines, it is the simplest and most secure for the client to decide the right measurements for the individual application. Additionally, this can dispense with any danger of "overdosing" of CBD. (Get familiar with CBD measurement)

It relies upon the malady.

Likewise, most clinical pictures treated with CBD require just generally little dosages. Just in intense instances of nervousness and seizure issue, for example, epilepsy is prescribed from the earliest starting point, to begin with moderately high measurements.

Focus on starting point and amount

Another significant factor in abstaining from overdosing with CBD is the starting point of the CBD. Engineered CBD regularly has an unexpected power in comparison to a similar measure of normally delivered CBDs. Amounts should, thusly, be considered with an attentive gaze.

What occurs with a cannabidiol overdose?

An overdose of CBD in the traditional sense, be that as it may, can't be normal in any case. Even though it is conceivable to take "to an extreme" CBD and therefore to satisfy the realities of an "overdose," even with such a CBD overdose, no negative impacts are known up until now. A couple of clients who took expanded

Brad J. Simon

dosages of CBD for test reasons grumbled uniquely of a marginally expanded sedation impact, which prompted exhaustion.

All things considered, there is no danger of taking an excessive amount of CBD. It can just happen that you take a superfluous measure of CBD and in this way no more impact expanding impact. In any case, an exemplary overdose more often than not never occurs.

CBD symptoms - are there reactions and collaborations?

The CBD can be utilized to treat an assortment of maladies is currently notable. In the same way as other natural cures, CBD may have symptoms or communications notwithstanding its useful impacts. Every individual responds distinctively to specific substances thus can't be barred from the beginning that there is a response after the CBD ingestion.

How sheltered is CBD?

Cannabidiol, casually known by the shortened form CBD, can help with a different issue. CBD is utilized to unwind, to discover light rest and rest through and, for instance, to stifle hunger. Be that as it may, CBD has a lot more advantages and advantages.

CBD items are typically utilized as enhancements or as a help for medicinal issues. Be that as it may, an ever-increasing number of competitors promise to a quicker recovery, with the assistance of CBD.

The inquiry emerges toward the start: Does CBD have symptoms? What's more, assuming this is the case, which ones? As the extent of CBD is wide, it is imperative to contemplate this issue intently and report conceivable symptoms.

With the goal that you can become familiar with the conceivable reactions of cannabidiol, we have assembled a short rundown. Be that as it may, CBD has few symptoms and is viewed as an amazingly protected substance.

What reactions can happen?

Cannabidiol has been characterized by numerous doctors and specialists as all around endured by past examinations. Reactions don't happen with ordinary utilization. This was additionally the consequence of a gathering of the World Health Organization's Expert Committee on Drug Addiction in November 2017. The wellbeing specialists assessed the recently known investigations on CBD. Here they reached the accompanying resolution:

CBD isn't psychoactive

- CBD is very much endured both by people and by creatures

- CBD does not represent a hazard to physical wellbeing

- CBD does not trigger reliance, neither physically nor rationally

The WHO additionally inspected the restorative capability of CBD at the gathering. They see enough proof that CBD is a viable medication for epilepsy. In the treatment of Alzheimer's, malignant growth, psychosis or Parkinson's, the cannabinoid may turn out to be progressively significant later on.

Because of the impact of explicit proteins, CBD may influence the ordinary working of the placenta. Hence, pregnant ladies should take cannabinoids, for example, CBD simply after the cautious conference with their primary care physician.

Rundown of known CBD symptoms

Influence on specific catalysts during pregnancy

- Low circulatory strain

- Inhibition of liver digestion

- Dry feeling in the mouth

- Increased tremor in some Parkinson's patients

- Increased languor

- Higher intraocular weight

- Trouble nodding off

- Limited craving

Conceivable reactions in detail

Brad J. Simon

By and large, one has the feeling that cannabis oil brings no huge reactions. Indeed, even in concentrates with extraordinarily high portions of CBD, no negative impacts were noted. Be that as it may, this data isn't yet totally solid - further examinations are as of now in advancement.

Better nod off gratitude to CBD

Once in a while, it is accounted for that the cannabinoid causes the contrary impact, in particular, a sleeping disorder. This reaction can be effectively anticipated if the admission of the separate CBD item does not happen at night. A generally excellent option is to drink a quieting hemp tea one hour before hitting the hay.

CBD oil during pregnancy

As noted above, an alert is prompted as CBD may meddle with complete placental capacity. In some cell tests, it has been discovered that CBD influences both the P-glycoprotein and the bosom malignant growth obstruction protein. Since these proteins assume a job in the smooth working of the placenta, it isn't prescribed to take CBD during pregnancy - even at low portions.

For this trial, grown-up zebrafish in Brazil got high dosages of CBD. There were standard instructional meetings that tried the memory of the fish. In particular, regardless of whether the memory of zebrafish under the customary impact of CBD worked more awful or possibly better, it was likewise found that the fish were less apprehensive.

Another gathering of fish got caffeine for a drawn-out period as a control gathering. The negative impacts portrayed were littler.

As we would like to think, the investigation isn't extremely significant on the grounds that the examination was performed on zebrafish whose conduct does not coordinate those of people. Be that as it may, this trial likewise demonstrated that CBD indicates basically no negative impact.

An expanded tremor in Parkinson's patients

Some Parkinson's patients report altogether more tremors in the wake of taking CBD, while others experience no crumbling. It is suggested that you counsel your primary care physician before taking CBD. By and large, a few examinations affirm that CBD may assume a critical job in Parkinson's throughout the following couple of years.

Dry inclination in the mouth

Another reaction of CBD is a dry mouthfeel, like the utilization of THC. This impact is brought about by the inclusion of the endocannabinoid framework (EBS) in hindering salivary generation. Enactment of specific receptors changes spit generation, which can prompt a dry mouth. Drinking a lot of water in the wake of taking it will help.

Low pulse

Higher dosages can prompt a slight fall in pulse. This typically occurs in almost no time of ingestion of the CBD. In the event that you are taking antihypertensive medicine, you ought to counsel your primary care physician before taking CBD. Notwithstanding, this symptom can frequently be settled by drinking some espresso or tea.

Laziness

At higher portions, CBD may cause sluggishness. Be that as it may, this reaction of CBD is scarcely archived and stays questionable. In the event that you become abnormally worn out in the wake of taking it, don't work apparatus or drive vehicles.

No reactions during ordinary use

These reactions of CBD oil have not been completely illustrated, and a metastasis concentrate found that CBD drops are alright for people and creatures. Cannabidiol was observed to be neither dangerous nor negative in untransformed cells.

Long haul contemplates as afterthought impacts of CBD don't yet exist - as needs are, no coupling articulations are made.

Shouldn't something be said about incomprehensible responses?

Brad J. Simon

Cannabis has a two-stage impact: there are the depicted and known parts of unwinding to enactment, with CBD, as referenced here, having a physical impact. Nonetheless, even with high portions or an extraordinary affectability of the customer, these sensations can be turned around! Neurosis and tension assaults are not as uncommon as it appears, however, these confusing impacts can without much of a stretch be precluded by the correct portion and some alert being used. There are reports that low dosages increment consideration and CBD is regularly possibly dosed higher when clients need to nod off.

CBD symptoms of low-quality items

The utilization of cannabidiol (CBD) is related to minor symptoms. Be that as it may, a potential wellbeing risk exists in low-quality CBD items. These can be tainted with synthetic compounds. Business CBD items are accessible in various quality. Sadly, it is hard for purchasers to know which items are reliable. An examination by Argon Canna in 2017 that the maker's data on the CBD substance of their items aren't generally to be trusted.

Customers can ensure themselves for the most part using natural CBD items. In this way, you are as of now erring on the side of caution that no pesticides or other substance added substances are incorporated into the CBD item. Additionally, obviously, ought to consistently be turned to a confided in the vendor. When all is said in done, pretty much every client on the Internet has a vendor who has practical experience in characteristic items and whose common cures are in generally excellent quality. Obviously, new things can be given it a shot, yet here you ought to tune in to the proposals of loved ones so you get great and high caliber. CBD reactions of inadequate items would thus be able to be rejected.

Cannabis is as yet a significant partner in an assortment of ailments and grievances. This likewise demonstrates it is presently utilized by an assortment, and the surveys on the Internet are reliably positive. Obviously, CBD symptoms, which are typically brought about by overdosage, can likewise happen. Beginning with little portions, however, is generally expected with the little reaction of CBD. Just the loss of hunger can be tricky, particularly in fundamentally sick individuals or individuals with bulimia, which is the reason CBD ought to be maintained a strategic distance from here.

CHAPTER:-3

HOW TO BUY CBD OIL: FINDING THE RIGHT PRODUCT?

O f course, you think the nature of your cannabis is significant. Regardless, you have to realize how to store concentrates and edibles appropriately. It's simple, and your reserve remains new.

You have discovered a specific cannabis train that you appreciate. It is actually what you were searching for and need to coordinate the strain into your life. You have purchased all that could be needed concentrate or edibles that you can use for a couple of months. On the off chance that that. By and large, you may have continued a bit too rapidly.

Brad J. Simon
The impact of wrong stored cannabis

When putting away cannabis, you would prefer only not to conceal it from supportive companions. It is likewise of imperative significance for keeping your concentrates and edibles new. We have aggregated a peril list for you with the hazard factors that can influence the extraordinary taste or nature of your concentrate if you don't store it appropriately:

- Moisture

- Direct light and a lot of daylight

- Heat sources

- Pollution

- Mildew or shape

- Insects

On the off chance that you simply leave cannabis someplace, it can get ruin inside a couple of days!

CAPACITY SOLUTIONS

E verybody has a most loved stockpiling technique. Cannabis can be put away for nearly time everlasting under immaculate conditions. Be that as it may, the capacity time relies upon the capacity strategy and the sort of item you use.

Silicone compartments: This is a perfect answer as long as possible. Attempt to discover a holder that is generally a similar size as the measure of concentrate to be put away. This diminishes the danger of dampness collecting in it.

Water/air proof holders: If you need to keep focuses well for a month, pack little amounts in the heating paper. At that point, you put the bundles in a huge ziplock sack. You do this in a compartment that you seal water/air proof.

Glass containers: Small glass containers, safeguarding containers and different glass holders are similarly reasonable. It depends a bit on what you need to keep.

Items that don't adhere to glass can without much of a stretch be put away in impermeable pots, which you set away in a dull spot or the cooling rack. If you need to keep your break, which is somewhat sticky, wrap it well in preparing paper; at that point, it doesn't adhere to the dividers of the compartment.

Solidifying: If you stop concentrates, you can frequently keep them for as long as a year. The quality and taste don't break down essentially. Notwithstanding, this requires some alert when bundling the concentrate. You should guarantee that there is no more air in it. Something else, dampness will develop in case of temperature changes. If you expel the concentrate from the cooler, let it defrost gradually. An abrupt change in temperature can influence the taste or even ruin your concentrate.

Storage Possibilities For Edibles

It is ideal to keep cannabis edibles in the ice chest. Particularly when they contain fixings, for example, oil, sugar, and flour. Edibles are helpless to shape and ruin rapidly if you store them at room temperature. This is fundamental because they more often than not contain a couple of additives.

When you purchase cannabis edibles, investigate the best before the date and the mark, so you know how you can best spare them. If conceivable, enclose them by wax paper or aluminum foil. Plastic bundling material can impact the taste. Put the enveloped edibles by a water/air proof holder, which you at that point store in your fridge.

TIPS

On the off chance that conceivable, don't utilize straightforward holders; cannabis is immediately influenced by direct light. Try not to utilize plastic sacks; they can't generally be hermetically fixed. Glass or silicone compartments are better.

Never store cannabis - the two concentrates and edibles - roundabout light.

If you are enveloping concentrates by preparing the paper to keep them, ensure you wear gloves. Along these lines, you avert the fats and microbes that are on your hands from being moved.

Your refrigerator is a phenomenal spot for putting away edibles, cannabis-enhanced oil, analgesic, and tinctures. Ensure they avoid the reach of youngsters!

Do, you regularly make a plunge the ice chest? Possibly you have some cash leftover for a minibar to keep your cannabis and edibles refrigerated. Along these lines, you counteract temperature vacillations. Note the bundling date on the cannabis concentrates and edibles. So you generally know when you pressed them.

Continuously purchase your items from solid vendors and dispensaries. At the point when the cannabis is offered in plastic or not bundled by any means, focus on the freshness of the item.

Attributes OF ruined CANNABIS

If you are uncertain whether your cannabis is put away effectively, check for the accompanying sign:

Buildup drops in the compartment

Obvious buildup and shape

Discoloration

Unscented cannabis

Items that vibe weak, unpleasant and dry

Things to see on the off chance that you need to store your CBD oil appropriately

1. Fend off the CBD from direct light

The most ideal approach to keep your CBD oil and different items in obscurity, dry, and cool spot. Cannabinoids like CBD last the coldest.

A storeroom is a typical spot to store CBD items. The refrigerator is another incredible spot to keep your CBD because it's considerably cooler. If you choose to leave your CBD oil in the cooler and you think the dropper is getting excessively thick, simply leave the container under boiling water, and you're prepared to go.

On the off chance that you utilize your CBD every day, abstain from putting your CBD oil and different items in the cooler. Regardless of whether CBD-based items are left in the cooler for quite a while, because this is the coldest spot in your home, it isn't useful to defrost your CBD consistently on the off chance that you wish to utilize it.

Utilize the cooler alternative for exceptionally long haul stockpiling of your CBD.

What you need to maintain a strategic distance from is presenting direct daylight to CBD oil, containers, and different items, (for example, on a counter close to a bright window), as this can bother the CBD.

2. Protect your items from the warmth

Warmth is another approach to splash your CBD stocks. Therefore, it is significant not to uncover your CBD items to extraordinary warmth. Try not to put the machine in cupboards close warmth transmitting apparatuses and don't open it to direct warmth (and light) from the sun.

Most CBD items are sent in sealed shut compartments (for instance, a make-up jug or mouthpiece) explicitly intended to avert presentation to air.

You can do your best to keep your CBD oil and different items in a similar bundle for which they were conveyed for quality confirmation purposes. After each utilization, watch that you have shut the bundling to avert any air passage.

3. Stay away from air contact

Much the same as light and warmth, air can influence your CBD.

Estimation of the powerful cost per milligram of CBD oil

The customary examination per cost per milligram

A speedy inquiry and you will discover numerous articles and adding machines online that are intended to enable you to look at the cost of CBD between brands. These sources pursue a fundamental equation that considers two straightforward components:

The cost of an item

The CBD content in this item

With this strategy, the customary value examination:

Push. Cost/CBD cont. in mg = cost per mg of CBD content

This examination is straightforward: take the cost and partition it by the absolute CBD substance of a specific item. They think about the item spectra, considering the cannabinoid and terpene substance of a specific concentrate.

Take our containers, for instance. The savviest choice is a 10-mg 30-check bottle (300 mg CBD content) for $ 39.95. With the assistance of this correlation, we play out the accompanying figuring:

39.95 USD/300 mg = 0.13 USD Price per mg of CBD content

Precisely right? Truly - BUT, here is an enormous piece that no one is discussing: bioavailability.

The ignored issue of bioavailability

Up to this point, practically all CBD items available had comparative oil-based cosmetics. Practically all cases and tinctures contain a full-range hemp concentrate, or CBD detach suspended in an oil transporter, for example, MCT oil. These transporter oils are not only for the show; they assume a key job in expanding the bioavailability of a specific item.

Bioavailability is the level of an item that has a functioning impact when devoured. This is the awful news: conventional oil-based cases have a normal bioavailability of under 10%. This implies 90% or a greater amount of the item you devour is flushed out of your body.

The issue is that when CBD oil cases are gulped, the item enters the digestive system and afterward needs to go through the supposed first-pass digestion. During this methodology, just a modest quantity of the item enters the circulatory system and ends up dynamic, while the rest is discharged as waste from the body.

CBD tinctures help battle this issue. Beneath the tongue, the hemp concentrate is consumed by the mucous films in the mouth before being gulped. This enables to some degree bypassing first to pass digestion

In the two cases, oil transporters, for example, MCT add to the retention - sublingual and gulped.

Water-solvent CBD oil: The Efficacy Gamechanger

The low potential issues were hard for some to swallow. Flushing over 90% of a valuable substance to the latrine is a long way from perfect. Accordingly, dynamic makers have built up a few new alternatives that altogether improve bioavailability contrasted with conventional oil-based items.

These items regularly alluded to as "water-dissolvable," have been exposed to new procedures that help to improve take-up in the body by up to 500%. There are a couple of various kinds available today, yet we will concentrate on the best: Nanoemulsions.

A Nano-emulsified item was exposed to a procedure of separating the oil particles into amazingly little pieces - a normal of 25 nanometers. Even though these particles are not water-dissolvable in the genuine sense, they are sufficient to scatter in fluids as opposed to sitting on them as oil. This procedure fundamentally builds the surface region of these oils and makes it simpler for the body to assimilate important cannabinoids and terpenes.

The count of as good as ever costs: the real cost per milligram

The value-adding machine is dependent on conventional grams dependent on the supposition: all items offer a comparative degree of bioavailability. This old truth is right over the road. As an industry, we should consider the maximum of an item.

To ascertain what we call the "compelling cost per milligram of CBD content" of an item. This examination considers the bioavailability, which better mirrors the absolute estimation of a specific item:

The cost of an item

The substance of the CBD in this

The bioavailability factor item

With our table above we can characterize the bioavailability factor of a specific item. This number speaks to the expanding variable of a specific item. Conventional items dependent on MCT-based oil is our reference to "1".

Oil-based items are our reason for an ingestion pace of 1x.

Liposomal items offer an ingestion pace of around 2 x.

The nanoémulsifiés items offer an account speed of around multiple times.

The new powerful cost per milligram is as

per the following:

(Item cost/CBD content in MG)/Bioavailability factor = powerful cost per milligram of CBD content

Take our first model through this new examination. With our containers, the least expensive choice is a jug of 30 10 mg tablets (content 300 mg CBD) for $ 39.95. Je nanoémulsionnés for a bioavailability factor 5. With this examination, we can play out the accompanying count:

($ 39.95/30 mg)/5 = viable cost of $ 0.03 per mg CBD

As should be obvious, this new correlation significantly affects the outcome: uncovering the real estimation of the item at a viable cost of $ 0.03 per milligram.

THE 10 BIGGEST CBD-BASED OIL ORGANIZATIONSION THE PLANET IN 2019

Science CV

The sciences CV is a leading manufacturer and supplier of hemp-based phyto-cannabinoids, including CBD oil, to the excellence, pet care, nutraceutical, specialty beverage, and food enterprises. Functional, just as the medication producer. Sciences CV has experienced impressive development and impressive profitability this year, exhibiting the strength of its products and brand awareness for the CBD petroleum industry. The PlusCBD product line is well-positioned for normal approval and across the board appropriation, with social and health sectors continuing to help CBD standardization and marketing. CV Sciences recently expanded its television business to a sum of 1968 natural stores, making it one of the biggest CBD oil companies on the planet.

MENDOZA

Endoca is one of the largest oil organizations in the CBD and exports the biggest number of CBD oil producers in Europe with a US branch. TheCompany cases to have manufactured products from certified organic and regular hemp plants (hemp), grown and grown without pesticides or herbicides. Endoca produces hemp products of the highest quality, including CBD oil and different cannabinoids, as there are more than 80 species in nature. The organization manufacture its factories, harvests, and processes them and supplies the completed products with its equipment and machines. The company also has its shipping and storage facilities. The next huge step for Endoca is to use solar vitality as a source of sustainable power source.

Gaia Botanicals

Bluebird Botanicals, also known as Gaia Botanicals, is one of the award-winning CBD oil organizations and one of the leading manufacturers of hemp-based CBD consumer products. Even though most sales are made on the web, their products are likewise sold in physical stores and at other outer retailers. The company has been marketing CBD products to other companies around the globe for many years and sells its pure extracts to organizations. Bluebird Botanicals right now has merchants in Japan, South America, and Europe. The company also works in different districts. Their products incorporate oil extricates, showers, CBD capsules and other pet items. Gaia Botanicals released new products in November 2016, CBD isolates and hemp shirts.

Isodiol International

Isodiol International has been developing pharmaceuticals, health, and wellness products for quite a while and is now generally supporting the pharmaceutical industry with its recently approved CBD items as a active fixing. The company is currently focusing on the health benefits of hemp and is effectively marketing hemp products and consumer solutions. Isodiol International is particular and perceived to identify the conceivable outcomes and patterns of all cannabinoids accessible in hemp. The company sells its extensive product portfolio through various directs in Germany and abroad.

Brad J. Simon
Medical Marijuana

Medical marijuana is an leader in mechanical hemp and cannabis products. The Company has turned into the market leader in CBD oil products explicitly for the nutraceutical, cosmeceutical, and pharmaceutical industries. Today, Medical Marijuana has several affiliates, including HempMeds, Managed Services for Wellbeing, Red Dice Holdings, CanChew Biotechnologies, Hempwire, Kannaway, HempVap, and HempMeds Brasil. In 2017, HempMeds Brasil, the auxiliary of Medical Marijuana, has received authorization from the Brazilian government to sell its products to treat people with autism range disorder (ASD), various sclerosis and Alzheimer's disease.

Aurora Cannabis (AC)

Aurora Cannabis is one of the world's best CBD oil organizations concentrated on manufacturing and selling therapeutic marijuana products. The award-winning organization also manufactures psychoactive products such as THC. Aurora Cannabis is to moved toward becoming the largest CBD producer with

570,000 kg for each year. With these facilities, the company can respond rapidly to the developing demand for CBD in Europe and other worldwide markets. Aurora cannabis already met GMP standards in the European Union through its 100% cannabis merchant Pedanios.

CBD American shaman

CBD American Shaman is a manufacturer of high-quality CBD grade oils. The organization has progressed toward becoming one of the largest organizations in the CBD market. CBD for the well-being of the world. The American Shaman CBD oils are exceptional and one of a kind. They are made with common and natural industrial materials that contain no GMOs, heavy metals or bug sprays and are 100% gluten-free. Their products incorporate hemp oil, CBD and terpene-rich hemp oil tinctures, skin care products, hemp oil for dogs and cats, high levels of cannabidiol (CBD) and, of course, pure CO_2 removes.

Canopy Growth Corporation

They are one of the leading medical marijuana companies that produce and sells CBD products through its understood Bedrocan. Bedrocan is one of the world's most experienced producers and exporters of legitimate medications. Canopy Growth Corporation as of late expanded its efforts to popularize therapeutic cannabis on the world market to Germany and Brazil. Bedrocan, a sativa cannabis plant; Bedropuur, tetrahydrocannabinol (THC) India for THC extraction, Bedica, an Indica prevailing variety of cannabis; Bedrobinol, Bediol, and Bedrolite items, the prevalent cannabis strains.

Elixinol

Elixinol is known for the production and creation of high quality characteristic and organic products. The Elixinol Group's portfolio consists of three primary fragments: Elixinol Australia, which focuses on medicinal cannabis, Hemp Foods Australia, which distributes food, and Elixinol USA, which sells healthful supplements. Elixinol USA is the lead company that makes and sells CBD nutraceuticals in the US market and other countries such as the US, Brazil, Japan, Puerto Rico, and the UK. Elixinol is the first company to dispatch a CBD product in Japan.

Today, The Company is pursuing a taught approach to drive development in Colorado.

IRIE CBD

They are one of the leading health and wellness items companies focused on providing natural health and wellbeing options as well as high-quality items. The CBD products come only from GMO-free, organically grown and sustainable to rich oils and terpenes.

Top CBD Brands IN EUROPE

This is how the two best CBD items have earned their positioning

We will probably give you an extensive, target review of the market for CBD items. Throughout this, we have set severe test criteria for the individual items, even though these may contrast negligibly relying upon the item classification (oil, fluid, containers, and so forth.).

Exclusive requirements were requested in the test however every item, in addition to other things as far as the immaculateness of cannabidiol, yet additionally, for instance, as far as generation strategies and accreditations.

Brad J. Simon

In like manner, we have just included items in this test are demonstrated to be sans THC, so don't have a psychoactive and inebriating impact. The therapeutic and medical advantages of cannabidiol are unmistakably in the frontal area, which is the reason our test criteria were as per the following:

Ingredients:

About the individual fixings and how to assess them. It likewise assumes a job with which CBD offer is worked and whether extra added substances have been utilized. The immaculateness and nature of the fixings have the top need and is in this way constantly top of the rundown.

Application:

In this part, we center around the one hand, the application, and then again, the ripeness of the item. The application may contrast altogether relying upon the item type, which is the reason we additionally indicate out you if you should require more frill. This is commonly the situation just with the fluids that are joined with evaporators and e-cigarettes. We additionally show how quick the impact happens and whether symptoms are not out of the ordinary. It additionally gives data on the flavor of the cannabidiol item.

Declarations and producer's guarantees: For you, we investigated what the maker guarantees and how he formally announces his item. Additionally, we record any seals that convey the item and have them incorporated into the test, including the last assessment.

Producer: For a therapeutic item like this, we figure is important to commit a different segment to the maker and his notoriety in the test. Thusly, you will get data about the maker, his brands, and how his notoriety is to be assessed.

The incentive for cash: Finally, we look at the dispassionately recorded subjective benchmarks, and the amount to the cost charged. To the extent that the item is accessible on Amazon, we arrange ourselves to the cost recorded there. Numerous CBD items, particularly oils, however, are sold legitimately from the producer and not on Amazon, at that point we orientate ourselves to the EIA and make the last decision.

Tributes: For our test, we perused the web for audits and surveys of the item. So you get target data from different purchasers and know ahead of time how fulfilled they were with an item and if there are any exceptional highlights to note.

CBD Hemp Oil - With 5, 15 or 20% CBD Share from Nordic Oil

Ingredient

The cannabidiol is a research facility tried CBD oil delivered in Germany, which is free of counterfeit additives, gluten, colors, and synthetic composts and development hormones. So companions of cannabidiol can depend on common, 100% unadulterated item.

The 5% variation contains 1.7 mg CBD; the 20% variation accompanies an estimation of 6.8 mg CBD.

The total rundown of fixings is organized as pursues:

- CBD (5%)

- Omega 3 unsaturated fats

- Omega 6 unsaturated fats

- Nutrient E

Terpene of the hemp plant

The item is along these lines truly appropriate for veggie lovers and vegetarians because of its fixings.

Application

Like each oil, the item from Nordic Oil is trickled under the tongue. The measurement can be balanced independently; the default is three drops that are dribbled under the tongue and afterward gulped - this can be rehashed up to three times each day. The ideal impact is accomplished if no fluids are flushed for the following 15 minutes after ingestion.

The beginning of activity is required following 10 to 15 minutes. The cannabidiol oil has, of course, a severely delayed flavor impression, which isn't as solid similarly as with numerous different oils. For the most part, the taste, as consistently with CBD oils, not delightful, however not irritating. A jug contains around 300 drops as per producer data.

Endorsements and producer's guarantees

The German maker has its CBD oil checked for immaculateness in a free lab. Additionally, Nordic Oil is liable to severe German and European eating regimen supplements. The producer guarantees an unadulterated item and can satisfy this guarantee as per the guided fixings.

Producer

Nordic Oil is a brand of Nordic Nutrition GmbH situated in Munich. The producer appreciates great notoriety on the Internet, likewise because it is one of only a handful couple of brands that really make the CBD oil in Germany and furthermore dispatched from Germany. This keeps on positively affecting the normal conveyance times. In general, there is nothing to grumble about, because Nordic Oil is a lead brand in the market of CBD items and furthermore different articles from the market of dietary enhancements.

Value execution proportion

CBD hemp oil variants with 5 or 15 or 20 percent CBD offer value/execution proportion contrasts relying upon the item. Our test champ is accessible with these three powers:

- 5% CBD

- 15% CBD

- 20% CBD

The EIA for the 5% oil is 49, - Euro, for the high dosed 20% oil, notwithstanding, 165, - Euro. Each of the three items is consistently marked down in cost and can be acquired legitimately from the maker less expensive. When all is said in done, it should likewise be viewed as that the value/execution proportion results from the CBD share. The higher-portion items are along these lines constantly less expensive than the 5% oil.

In general, the value/execution proportion can be evaluated "great," particularly for higher-portion variations.

The cost is somewhat higher than certain contenders, however, this is added because you purchase at Nordic Oil in Germany made items with incredible quality.

Conclusion

Nordic Oil has won the champ's honor with its 5, 15 or 20% CBD hemp oil. The cannabidiol item is 100% characteristic and unadulterated, abstained from all substances that have nothing to do with CBD oils is as yet made in Germany simultaneously. For the individuals who need to spend more on a superb CBD oil, the Nordic Oil item is the best decision. There is no chance to get around the German maker from Munich, particularly from German clients.

Focal points

Made in Germany

available in three forces

- Delivery from Germany

- without sketchy added substances

- suitable for vegetarians

- often accessible at a marked down cost from the producer

- excellent shop

- With profitable amino acids and nutrient E.

Disadvantage

Not the least expensive items in the market

Fixings

Accessible is the cannabidiol containers of the brand Nordic Oil with a CBD substance of 4% or 10%. For amateurs, we prescribe beginning with the low-portion item once more, yet if you as of now have the understanding and might want to reserve, you can utilize the 10% cases. The harvest utilized is again naturally unadulterated and was thusly not distorted with manures, additives, gluten, colors, or different added substances. Therefore, the containers have indistinguishable top-notch gauges from those found on our test champ.

The total rundown of fixings is given by the maker as pursues: Olive oil as an auxiliary bearer

CBD

Terpene from hemp

Hamburger gelatin for the containers

Glycerin

Water

As can be seen from the rundown, the containers are not reasonable for veggie lovers and vegans because of the case shell made of the gelatin from hamburger. Then again, on the off chance that you don't have such confinements, you can securely utilize them as a choice to oil.

Application

A Nordic Oil can accompany 60 cases, each containing roughly 6.4 mg CBD (in the 4% variation). The maker prescribes the admission of three cases for every day, in the first part of the day, around early afternoon and after supper. On the off chance that vital, the portion might be decreased or expanded somewhat. Nordic Oil additionally expresses that mix with greasy sustenances is prescribed as it accelerates the admission. With an effect of the impact is normal after around 30 minutes.

The beginning of activity is correspondingly longer contrasted with CBD oil since the case normally just needs to break down in the stomach before the fixings are then additionally disseminated. The taste does not make a difference, because these cases are gulped down. This makes them particularly for individuals to a solid option, which can't warm up to the regular taste of CBD oil, on the cannabidiol however does not have any desire to manage without.

Declarations and producer's guarantees

The producer from Munich guarantees an organically unadulterated item where the harvest was not affected by science. Similarly, no synthetic concoctions are utilized in the containers themselves. So also, the maker guarantees that with a container to 4% CBD substance, a comparable impact is accomplished as a drop from the 15% oil. As a result, you will get more CBD than the low-portion 5% oil. Once more, the creation was checked by a free research center to guarantee and affirm the quality.

Maker

As of now in the area of the test victor, we have managed the brand Nordic Oil. The items are made and disseminated by Nordic Nutrition GmbH in Munich, convey the seal "Made in Germany" by and by and are additionally transported from Bavaria. Both the brand and the producer behind it are a sign of superb quality.

CBD cases Nordic Oil 10 percent value execution proportion

As per the prescribed admission, one container of CBD cases from Nordic Oil will keep going for around three weeks. The MSRP for the 4% cases is 40, - Euro, for the 10% cases 80, - Euro. The two items are as common frequently with a markdown, which is deducted straightforwardly from the maker.

Who purchases the higher-portion containers can spare a little since you get a great deal more CBD per Euro contributed. Once more, it must be said that the

Nordic Oil items are unquestionably not the least expensive choices available, yet they dazzle with generation in Germany and top of the line quality.

Client audits

The containers from Nordic Oil are similarly also gotten as the recently depicted oil, which we have named test champ.

Aficionados of cannabidiol appear in gatherings and on different stages. Energetically of the high German quality and quick delivering, which likewise happens from Germany.

Conclusion

The CBD containers with 4% or 10% CBD substance are an extraordinary option for the individuals who can't warm up to the unpleasant taste of the oil. Since they are gulped down, they are true bland. Because of the gelatin utilized, they can be gulped simultaneously without incredible issues. The fantastic quality is deserving of the second spot in our extraordinary examination, the value/execution proportion is on a moderate to a decent level, contingent upon the chose measurement. Apprentices and experienced settle on with the selection of cases ensured nothing incorrectly!

Preferences

Made in Germany

Unadulterated CBD in natural quality

Accessible in two distinct powers

Created in a delicate procedure

Quick sending from Germany

Frequently accessible with a markdown from the maker

Safe shopping and administration request hotline at Nordic Oil

Burden

Isn't appropriate for veggie lovers and vegetarians

In low dose somewhat increasingly costly

Best CBD Oil for Sleep, Anxiety, Pain, and Insomnia

NuLeaf Naturals

Features

Contains a total range of cannabinoids and synergistic terpenes

Quick and free sending all things considered

A bigger number of faultfinders than anybody in the business

Various fixations (240 mg to 4,850 mg)

5 ml/240 mg (0.16 USD per mg)

NuLeaf Naturals has been focused on creating amazing CBD oils since 2014. NuLeaf Naturals, one of the most seasoned and best-evaluated organizations in the business, has set up itself as a trusted CBD producer. Outer research centers test every one of their items, and their profile in cannabinoids is noteworthy. They offer a special focus run for their natural CBD items extending from 240 mg to 4850 mg.

NuLeaf Naturals CBD oils spread all the range. It is 100% natural and is never produced with herbicides, pesticides, or synthetic composts. The brand likewise offers a full-range pet CBD oil tincture. NuLeaf Naturals offers free conveyance to every one of the 50 states. The brand's items are additionally sold at more than 1,000 points of offer all through the nation.

Useful for:

Sleepers with mellow to direct rest issue

CBD clients who need unadulterated CBD oil with no extra fixings

Clients of a full CBD range

Individuals with incessant torment or tension issue

PlusCBD oil - most noteworthy quality

Features

- "Gold Formula" full-range oil

- Sans GMO, vegan and without gluten

- 3 flavors

- Variable fixations (250 mg to 1500 mg)

- 1 oz/250 mg (0.15 USD per mg)

As one of the first since forever organizations to create CBD items in the US, they are one of the most persuasive voices in hemp resistance and have more retail space than any other individual.

This color is marked "Gold Formula," a full-range mix of terpenes, phytocannabinoids, unsaturated fats, and nutrient E. The drops are accessible in three qualities: 250 mg for each 1 oz. With or 750 mg and 1500 mg in 2 oz. Compartment. Likewise, CBD oil prescribes taking a large portion of a pipette or 15 drops for each portion. The drops are veggie lover well disposed and contain no GMO, gluten, or glycerin.

Notwithstanding a taste-unbiased adaptation of the drops is likewise accessible in the kinds of peppermint and goji berries, which are ideal for blending with beverages. Nourishing data for the three flavors can be found on the PlusCBD Oil site. The drops are generally shoddy and cost contingent upon the fixation, not more than 0.15 USD per mg. The brand offers quick conveyances to the United States and an assortment of universal goals.

Useful for:

- Individuals with moderate to serious manifestations of sleep deprivation

- The individuals who incline toward CBD colors

- CBD clients who incline toward non-enhanced or seasoned oils

- Clients of full range CBD items

- Cbd® - Best Value

Features

- Wide scope of oil fixations (300 mg - 5000 mg)

- Best accessible cost

- Colors, containers, topical and suppositories

- 30 ml/300 mg (0.10 USD per mg)

CBD oil-based commodities can be very costly, which can be an obstruction for individuals looking for treatment or easing of different maladies and disarranges. Cbd® is a prominent value special case. cbd® offers amazing, sans the oils in an assortment of fixations (300 mg to 5000 mg) just as in sizes (30 ml and 60 ml). The cost of these oils is $ 29.99 for 300 mg oils and $ 99.99 for 1500 mg oils. These costs are well underneath normal.

Notwithstanding CBD oils, cbd® offers topical creams for the skin, shower bombs (we prescribe to attempt them), cases and pills, splash oils and pet items. These items are affordable contrasted with the challenge. With cbd®, clients can restore the products inside 30 days of the primary request for a full discount.

Useful for:

Sleepers with indications of mellow to direct a sleeping disorder

The individuals who favor topical containers and oils

CBD clients who incline toward items without THC

Individuals with ceaseless agony and nervousness issue

Spruce - Maximum execution

Features

- Full range oil with 0.3% THC and other characteristic cannabinoids

- Treated from natural hemp seed oil

- Veggie lover and sans gluten

Brad J. Simon

- 2,400 mg focus

- 30 ml/2400 mg ($ 0.11 per mg)

CBD-rich oils are especially appropriate for individuals with serious torment, a sleeping disorder, interminable torment, uneasiness/gloom indications, and different conditions that require more grounded impacts. Our first decision in this classification is proficient evaluation spruce CBD oil in a 30 ml container with a grouping of 2,400 mg. Each drop of oil contains around 80 mg of CBD, a powerful portion for individuals with distress or serious side effects.

The taste-nonpartisan oil is removed from natural hemp seed oil. It is viewed as a veggie lover and sans gluten and contains no improving or additives. The oil contains 0.3% THC, which implies that individuals who are tried for medications might not have any desire to take it, yet this generally limited quantity delivers next to zero psychoactive impact. The cost per mg is $ 0.11, which makes CBD Spruce Lab Grade Oil better than expected.

Useful for:

Individuals with extreme side effects of a sleeping disorder, perpetual agony, and uneasiness issue

The individuals who lean toward CBD colors

CBD clients who lean toward enhanced oils

Clients of Spectrum CBD items

CBD Oil Recipes for Home - Healthy Cooking and Baking With CBD

CBD in the kitchen: the fundamentals

The phytocannabinoids must be enacted before cooking to be compelling. This procedure is classified as "decarboxylation." So if CBD blooms are utilized as beginning material, they should initially be treated with warmth before they are reasonable for further handling.

For this, the blooms can essentially be put on a preparing sheet and warmed at 110-120 degrees for an hour.

On the off chance that this readiness is too tedious, it can likewise utilize instant items, for example, CBD oil or concentrate for certain plans.

Brad J. Simon

At that point, you simply must be mindful so as not to overheat the CBD to get the impact.

So if the blossoms are enacted or the last items are prepared, the cooking can begin!

Crude nourishment with the additional power: the avocado radish bowl

If you need to misuse the wellbeing improving impacts of CBD completely, it is best joined with the nutrients, follow components and fiber from vegetables and natural products.

It bodes well to pick a CBD oil with hemp oil as a bearer oil. This makes the oil Omega 3.

Together with avocado, radishes, pomegranate seeds, and sprouts, it turns into a new taste experience loaded with surface and fragrance.

The quinoa is filling and loaded with fiber. The way that the bowl is cold or tepid, it can likewise be astounding as a lunch out and about or in the workplace to be readied. The CBD has no psychoactive impact so it very well may be expended during the day without variations from the norm.

You need:

- 1 avocado

- 1 cup quinoa

- 6 radishes

- 50 g of sprouts of your decision

- ½ head seasoned lettuce (eg sheep's lettuce)

- ½ pomegranate

- 6 tbsp. CBD oil

- 4 tbsp. apple vinegar

- Salt and pepper to taste

Planning:

Cook quinoa after the bundle handout. Cut the avocado into vertical strips. Mince the radishes into little 3D squares. Wash the lettuce and hack it to taste. Center the pomegranate. In a compartment, blend the oil and apple juice vinegar and add salt and pepper to taste.

Once the quinoa is cooked, channel and spot in a profound bowl.

At that point wrap the lettuce, the radishes, and the pomegranate and gorgeously enhance the avocado. Sprinkle the sprouts liberally over the dinner and pour the dressing over the completed feast when it is eaten.

For a decent begin to the day: A green smoothie with CBD

Frequently, the trademark CBD taste may take some becoming accustomed to. An incredible method to make day by day consumption a genuine feature is a green smoothie with CBD. The flavor of the vegetables and organic products, the CBD taste is moderated and barely perceptible at a typical portion of, for instance, 5-10 drops of CBD remove the multi-day.

Required for the super smoothie:

- ½ cucumber

- 1 bunch of spinach

- 1 banana

- 2 sticks of celery

- The possess portion of CBD

- 4 stems Mint

Discretionary: Chia seeds, flax seeds, sunflower seeds, acai berries and so forth.

Readiness:

It is prescribed to "layer" the fixings from firm to delicate to accelerate the blending procedure. So put the strong fixings like celery and cucumber and banana in the blender first and afterward layer the spinach, the CBD, the mint and the discretionary seeds or natural products.

Blend, empty the smoothie into your preferred glass or a reusable jug and appreciate.

The most loved plunge reinterpreted: Guacamole with CBD

We as a whole love our guacamole, regardless of whether it's bread or tasty corn tacos. The avocado, tomatoes, and onions are tasty as well as sound. On the off chance that you might want to enhance the adjusting and to fortify the impact of the CBD with this incredible plunge, you can supplant the olive oil with hemp oil with CBD.

To set you up, need:

- 1 avocado

- 1 tomato

- ½ red onion

- 2 tbsp hemp oil

- The individual CBD portion of

- salt and pepper to taste

- 4 stalks of smooth parsley

Arrangement:

Pulverize the avocado with a fork. This keeps a pleasant surface and still gets rich. At that point include the hemp oil or completed CBD oil blended with your portion of CBD and blend again with the avocado. Cut the tomato into little solid shapes. Finely grind the onion and overlap in both. Season with salt and pepper. Slash the cover parsley and sprinkle up the completed guacamole.

Heating with CBD

The crude sustenance and CBD plans are genuine wellbeing support for the body and soul. Be that as it may, once in a while it might likewise be a little sin. Heated merchandise, for example, biscuits, cakes, or brownies are best heated alone, and by setting them up at home, you can likewise add wellbeing elevating segment to the sweet baked goods.

When heating with CBD, it is first essential to expel the CBD from the blossoms. It is prudent to break up the fat-dissolvable substance in spread or margarine. For the planning of this CBD margarine, there are various strategies, every one of which gives distinctive temperature cycles. The essential standard is, in any case, consistently the equivalent:

The spread or margarine is set in a pot together with generally hacked, enacted CBD blooms and the warmth breaks up the CBD and goes into the spread.

On the off chance that that is excessively costly, you can likewise utilize CBD oil. In the two cases, it is significant when preparing not to warm the stove higher than 145-150 degrees. Something else, the significant CBD essentially dissipates. All in all: If the temperatures like to analyze! You can likewise interface a lower temperature with longer preparing time.

It is ideal, to begin with, a lower temperature first and to get to the perfect temperature yourself. The gentler the readiness, the better!

Dull Brownies with CBD

Brownies don't need to be unfortunate calorie bombs. With a couple of stunts and solid fixings, the delightful chocolate cakes are sweet, smooth, and similarly as heavenly as the ordinary calorie bombs.

To set you up, need:

- 1 container of dark beans, depleted weight 250 g

- 2 eggs

- 5 set dates

- 50 g cocoa powder

- 80 ml maple syrup

- Optional 1 teaspoon vanilla concentrate

- ½ teaspoon soft drink

- 1 squeeze of salt

A sum of 120 g spread, of which the extent with the ideal dose as CBD margarine (Eg, 20 g of CBD margarine and 100 g of ordinary spread) or the ideal measure of CBD separate in the fluid margarine give

80 g of walnuts

Planning:

Preheat the broiler to a limit of 150 degrees.

Spread a heating tin of around 25 × 25 with preparing a paper or simply oil it.

Soften the margarine in a water shower. Cleave up depleted beans, dates, eggs, cocoa powder, maple syrup, vanilla concentrate, soft drink and salt in a blender and blend well. At that point empty the spread into the mixture while the blender keeps on running. Presently the CBD concentrate can be included if no CBD spread was utilized.

At that point put the mixture in the form and smooth it by delicately shaking it. Slash the walnuts generally and afterward spread on the mixture.

Heat for around 30-40 minutes. After around 20 minutes, check how the brownies create and afterward glance around at interims of around 5 min.

Expel from broiler when the surface is somewhat broken, and the batter is firm.

At that point enable the baked good to cool totally.

The world's best banana bread - with CBD

The banana bread formula isn't just free of sugar and white flour yet additionally wealthy in fiber thus flavorful that it will be eaten in a matter of moments.

The appended CBD gives the solid nibble an adjusting and wellbeing advancing impact. Impeccable as a little breakfast or sound option in contrast to espresso.

You need:

- 275 g spelled flour

- 2 tsp preparing powder

- 1 tsp cinnamon

- 1 squeeze salt

- 50 g vegetable milk

- 40 g coconut oil

Wanted portion CBD extricate

On the other hand 40g CBD margarine or spread in the proportion of the ideal measurements

3-6 set dates (contingent upon the ideal level of sweetness)

4 overripe bananas

Readiness:

Preheat the oven to a limit of 150 degrees.

Coconut oil softens. Mix spelt flour, heating powder, cinnamon and salt in a bowl. Puree plant milk and dates. Pound 3 ½ of the bananas with a fork. Blend banana wheat, date milk glue, and the dry fixings. At that point include the ideal portion of CB separate.

Include the coconut oil and blend everything. Put the batter into a lubed tin, smoothen it out and cut the remainder of the banana half the long way and press it down into the mixture with the round side down for improvement.

At that point heat the bread for a sum of as long as an hour, search just because following 40 minutes.

Expel from the broiler, permit to cool and appreciate.

Kill Devil Hills Library
East Albemarle Regional Library
Kill Devil Hills, NC 27948
252-441-4331
5/2021

CPSIA information can be obtained
at www.ICGtesting.com
Printed in the USA
LVHW080009170919
631311LV00005B/274/P

9 781686 080890